Drug Tested for Being Happy

True Stories to Make You Laugh

Drug Tested for Being Happy

True Stories to Make You Laugh

Kathy Thorson Gruhn

For information about other books or performances.
Go to: kathythorsongruhn.com
or
mybabycompass.com

Layout and Editing by Maureen Ryan Griffin
Cover Photo by Steve Reisch Photography

Manufactured in the United States
MBC Publishing
289 Green Fields Lane
Columbus, NC 29722

ISBN 978-0-9844085-5-9
ISBN 978-0-9844085-6-6 (eBook)

I would like to dedicate this book to
the people in my life that felt
I had the ability to make it happen:

Dr. William Gruhn,
Jack Canfield,
and
Maureen Ryan Griffin

Table of Contents

Introduction

I wrote this book, first of all, because I love to see people laugh. As a speech pathologist, I spent years helping people regain their speech, which was very rewarding. Language is the means to love and connection, and these are important to all human beings.

When we speak, we take turns—or that is what we're supposed to do. Those with an ego problem tend to interrupt or just never stop talking, disregarding proper etiquette. However, when we laugh, we laugh together. No ego. No worries. No high blood pressure. No anxiety.

Some of these stories are about my husband Bill. I wrote them this past year to help me get through the sadness I felt as he was dying. They made me laugh and remember the crazy times we've had together and I didn't want to forget them. That's another reason for writing this book—and a great reason for you to write down your own happy stories. It's a cathartic, healing way for you to get through rough times.

Bill wasn't always fond of my stories—probably because he had to hear them more than once or because he was the fall guy, which put him in a bad light.

However, when my husband became ill, he looked forward to hearing whatever funny story I'd written each week. Laughing eased the pain of his inevitable death. Sometimes a nurse would overhear my storytelling and join us. When the laughter subsided, the next thing I would hear was, "Is that true?"

Bill and I would look at each other, nod our head yes and begin to laugh all over again.

I also wrote this book because I've been telling stories my whole life. What else was there to do for entertainment in tiny Blooming Prairie, Minnesota, where we didn't even have a movie theatre? Not even a stoplight. We were responsible for our own entertainment.

I grew up in a storytelling circle of relatives around our dining room table. At every holiday, I'd hear stories about my family I'd heard many times before and we would laugh before we even got halfway through the story. We didn't need to hear the ending. We knew it. The only problem was when we had company who didn't know the punch line. They'd quietly sit like bumps on a log with fake smiles frozen on their faces, trying to figure out what was so funny.

I call these stories "true stories" because many of them are so ridiculous that people have trouble believing them. They don't seem to have trouble remembering them though. People will remind me about a story I told at a party many years ago and ask me to retell it. If I remember it, I'm happy to. And if I don't, I just tell them a new Ole and Lena joke and they're usually satisfied with that.

I'm from Minnesota and I grew up listening to *Prairie Home Companion,* which poked gentle fun at people of Scandinavian descent. After all, there are so many of us living there.

We all share a love of Ole and Lena jokes—we don't mind poking fun at ourselves. But sometimes I have to explain this Norwegian husband and wife who are staunch, conservative and a little slow-minded to non-Minnesotans.

Let me give you an example:

Ole: "Lena. We are finally married after dating twenty-nine years. I have the most beautiful honeymoon suite in Minneapolis, Minnesota. The drive is only two hours."

Lena: "Oh, Ole, you know I've been saving myself for ya. Tell me about the honeymoon suite."

Ole: "It has a king size bed, a Jacuzzi and a mirror on the ceiling. Why don't you sit a little closer to me here in the front seat?"

Ole starts rubbing Lena's thigh. Lena's heart starts beating faster and faster. She's breathing heavily and isn't sure she can make it to Minneapolis.

Lena: "Please, Ole, you can go farther!"

So Ole took Lena to Canada. Ya, you betcha by golly.

If they're not satisfied with that joke, I have many more up my sleeve.

I've been telling funny stories to my writing group for almost ten years. My writing coach, Maureen Ryan Griffin, has been asking me all along to write them down and put them in a book. She's thrilled that I finally took on this project.

I changed some names and locations in the stories to protect the not-so-innocent. It doesn't matter that much, my home town will know who they are.

Now, I have these true stories to share with you. Laughing isn't the only route to happiness, so some of the stories are just warm memories I wanted to share. I hope at least a few of these tales make you laugh and that reading them makes you happy.

Drug Tested for Being Happy

Being happy can get you in terrible trouble. It can even get you drug tested three times. But there is an upside. You get a story.

And if you're not only happy, but totally accident prone, practically completely uninhibited, and strongly inclined to attract mishaps, well, then you get enough true stories—whether people believe them or not—to write a book. So, let me start with the story of how I once got drug tested for being happy—the book will go on from there.

At the time, I was working as a speech pathologist in a developmental day care in Charlotte, North Carolina. I loved my job and the staff I was working with.

Well, most of the staff. There was one woman, our director's secretary, who had worked there for over twenty years—she was grumpy. But even though I didn't exactly like her, I took it upon myself to try to make her happy. I finally succeeded by finding her a physician she loved who happened to be a good friend of mine.

Unfortunately, not long after she started her new doctor, he moved his practice to South Carolina and his services no longer qualified for her insurance. (I'm not so sure she wasn't the reason for his move. I was married to a doctor and know that a grumpy, demanding patient can make a physician's life miserable. It can make his family miserable, also.)

I didn't realize that my secretary friend thought her healthcare was my responsibility until the morning she asked, "Have you found me another doctor yet?" as I was collecting my mail.

"You know, I don't even have a doctor myself. Have you tried the Family Physicians on Cedar Avenue? They're good."

"I don't like them. They make me see different doctors. I want one doctor to take care of me."

"Medicine has changed over the years and I think you may have to go with the flow," I said.

"I want a doctor like the last one you found me. I loved him. He catered to me."

"Sorry, I didn't realize when I said 'I do' to my husband that along with 'for better and worse' came 'and find a doctor for anyone that asks,' " I said jokingly.

Well, she didn't find it funny. If looks could've killed, I'd be dead. Our relationship went downhill after that conversation.

A few weeks went by. Like always, I came to work with new jokes and stories to tell the staff at lunchtime. Laughter seemed to help with bonding and the stress of taking care of children with special needs.

I was in the middle of a story one day when my director walked into our breakroom. "Kathy, could you come in my office for a minute?"

"Sure, no problem. Let me tell the teacher in the three-year-old classroom I'll be a few minutes late."

When I walked into the director's outer office, I smiled at the grumpy secretary, who for the first time in months smiled back.

After ushering me in and closing the door to her inner office, the director said, "Kathy, I have a problem. My secretary requested that you be drug tested because you're always laughing and acting silly."

I could tell she was embarrassed to be making this request. "Are you serious? That woman hates me even though I've been bending over backwards to help her. Sure, give me the cup and I'll take care of it right now."

"That's not how it works. I give you these forms and you have to report to a testing center in downtown Charlotte. You can leave an hour early from work today."

"No problem. I'll take care of it. What else is that witch going to do to make my life miserable?"

"Sorry, I haven't been here that long and she threatened to go over my head because we're friends."

"I don't blame you. Heck, it's fine with me. I'm getting off work early."

As I walked out of her office, I heard the secretary ask, "Did your meeting go well?" It was all I could do to keep myself from making an unkind gesture.

I left work early and headed to downtown Charlotte. This was in the year 2000 and drug testing was just beginning to become widespread. I was aware that the hospital and clinics I worked at sometimes gave random tests, but I'd never known anyone who was ever tested. I never had, and had no idea how the process worked.

I found the testing center, which was located in a double wide trailer in a shady part of town. I entered and immediately felt out of place in my suit, nylons, pumps and pearls. Orange jumpsuits ruled. I saw some chairs across the room and walked over to sit down.

A woman came up to me and asked to see my paper work. "You can't sit here," she said. "These seats are reserved for doctors and nurses that are randomly tested and who have an appointment. You are a suspect and you have to sit over there." She pointed to the seats next to the policeman and inmates.

The inmates looked at me, slightly taken aback. Maybe they thought I was a kingpin in the drug trade. I waited as people with appointments came and went. Finally, I was called.

The woman took me in a back room and instructed me to place my items in a locker. She then told me she had to pat me down.

"What are you looking for?" I asked.

"Urine," she said as she started patting down my leg.

"I'm not incontinent," I said, utterly naïve.

"Other people's urine."

"Why would I pay for someone else's drug test? It costs enough as it is."

That poor woman must have thought she hit the jackpot when it came to stupid. "In case you tried to pass someone else's urine as your own so you could pass the test," she said.

"Gross. You couldn't pay me enough to handle someone's urine."

"Yea, sure, heard that before. Follow me."

We went to a small bathroom and she proceeded to give me instructions. "Here's the specimen cup and the label. To take the specimen, wipe your genitals with these wipes, begin to urinate, take the specimen mid-stream, clean yourself off and place the cover on the specimen bottle. Peel off the label, stick it on the cup and put it behind the door that's labeled 'A'. Wrap the specimen with a towel. Do not flush the toilet. Do not put anything in the toilet. The wipes go in the waste paper basket."

She then sprayed blue-colored liquid in the toilet bowel. "Don't flush," she said.

"Where's the toilet paper?" I asked.

"There's no toilet paper. Use the wipes and don't put them in the toilet."

She walked out and I heard the door lock behind her.

I reviewed all of the directions as I opened the wipes. Women don't have the same advantage as men. It's a guessing game as to where that mid-steam is headed. Afterwards, out of habit, I flushed, but I wasn't worried. I'd done everything else right.

She knocked on the door. "Finished yet?"

"Yep, all done."

She entered the door like a little henchman and walked over to the toilet. "You flushed," she said as she stared into the toilet.

"Yeah, out of habit. The specimen is behind door 'A', which reminds me of the show *Let's Make a Deal.* Which door do you want?" I asked, hoping to see a smile.

"I can't accept your specimen. You flushed," she said without the smile. "The color in the toilet needs to turn green so I know that the specimen is fresh."

"You searched me. Go feel the specimen. It's warm."

"You'll have to come back tomorrow. You'll have to pay again."

I couldn't believe I was going to have to go through this again, all because I flushed.

When I got to work the next day, I walked into my director's office and told her what happened. We had a good laugh over my failure and she said I could leave work early again today. I'm sure the scuttlebutt around the office was that I didn't pass my drug test, but I didn't care. I headed out to my new hangout in downtown Charlotte that I had dubbed The Pee Palace.

"I'm back and here is my paperwork," I said. The same stern woman took it from me and pointed to the seats next to the prisoners.

"I know. I'm a suspect," I said. Again, I got strange looks from the crowd.

When my name was called, we went through the same procedure, including the pat down. My 'new friend' had had more physical contact with me in the last two days than my husband.

She led me back to the bathroom and proceeded to repeat the instructions. Again she told me to not flush the toilet.

"Got it. I have this down pat. I will not flush the toilet. In fact, I have such a fear now that I'm not sure if I'll ever be able to flush a toilet ever again," I said, hoping to see a smile.

No response whatsoever from her.

I followed the directions to a tee. As I was putting the cover on the specimen cup, out of nowhere there was a loud bang on the door, paired with a shrill "Don't flush the toilet." It scared me, causing me to lose my grip on the urine cup, which flew into the air, spilling urine down the front of my dress and all over the sink and floor.

"Damn, I just spilled urine everywhere," I yelled.

She came in the door, checked the unflushed toilet, and looked at the specimen cup.

"That isn't enough urine for me to check. Do you think you can give me another specimen in ten to twenty minutes? We have a water jug in the waiting room. We close at five."

"Excuse me, but don't you see that I'm covered in urine? I'm supposed to sit in the waiting room and wait for my bladder to fill? Really? Maybe you have a lost and found with some extra orange jumpsuits for me to change into so I can feel like part of the crowd."

Darn! I realized as soon as I said it that this was not the time to get smart.

I decided I had better be on my best behavior. "Sorry that I spilled urine all over the place. Give me some paper towels and Clorox and I'll clean it up. By the way, my bladder is like a camel. I'm not the typical woman that has to pee all the time, but for you I'll try." I went to the waiting room and drank two bottles of water with no luck.

"You'll have to come back tomorrow, but I won't charge you," she said. I could tell she was feeling a little guilty.

As I sat in Charlotte rush-hour traffic, I felt the urge to pee very badly. Where was that specimen cup when I needed it? It was a miserable ride home and I was doing the pee-pee dance all the way into the house.

I called the office the next morning and took the day off, not wanting them to know I was going for a urine test for the third time. Too embarrassing, even for me!

I headed to the lab and completed the process with no problem. A week later the results came back and I was fine, but I was pissed (no pun intended) at that secretary and spent a few days trying to figure out what I could do to make HER life miserable. But life's too short to hold onto grudges, and I soon forgot all about it.

Well, not completely. Good Friday came along a few months later and school was closed. My husband needed help in his research lab and so I went to work with him to help out. As I was labeling the syringes and specimen cups and packing the labs to be picked up, I had an inspired idea. I hid an unused specimen cup in my purse and took it home.

On our first day of work after the holidays, I came in early and placed the specimen cup, which I'd filled with lemonade, on the secretary's desk with a note that read: 'If you want to be happy; drink this.'

I heard a scream from her office a little while later, and shortly afterward, the director was standing at my door.

"Kathy. There's a urine sample on the secretary's desk. Only you would write a note like that. If it's yours, remove it," she said sternly.

With the director in tow, I went to the secretary's desk. Smiling at the grumpy old lady, I unscrewed the lid and took a swallow. "It's just lemonade," I said. "Want a swig?"

Growing Up in Blooming Prairie

Ham-It-Up Hamster

One day, while playing records on my small, shiny, red record player that I received for my eighth birthday, I had a bright idea. Why not let my hamster, Squeak, run on a record while it played? Wouldn't he like a break from the squeaky hamster wheel in his cage? I certainly didn't want to mess up my own "Over the Rainbow" record, so I used Mom and Dad's Glenn Miller album that had a few too many scratches on it already anyway. It was a 33 1/3 LP, so it gave Squeak plenty of room. The record was so old that it appeared to wobble while it played the last song, "In the Mood."

I was right. Squeak loved it and I knew he did. Whenever he heard "In the Mood," he would start gnawing on his door—his signal that he wanted to get out and run on the record while it played. I was amazed that he recognized the song and what to do. I was so proud of Squeak. I had the smartest hamster on the block.

Squeak was so good that one day I decided to challenge him and place him on a faster record—a 45

RPM. I inserted the yellow plastic adapter into "Somewhere Over the Rainbow" and stuck it on the turntable. (After all, Squeak was a pro now—the minute I picked him up from out of his cage his little legs started running in the air, ready for his record-landing.)

I carefully held Squeak over the record and put him down. What I hadn't thought of was that the record was much smaller, and that the arm stretched across the whole record, not just the last song of the LP. Squeak was "Somewhere Over the Rainbow" after less than a second. As soon as his little feet hit, he started running sideways and was flung into the air.

I looked everywhere for him, with no luck. I talked my little brother into helping me look, but Squeak was gone.

We didn't tell Mom or Dad what happened, and left the cage open for him to hopefully find his way back home. I don't know if he was so mad at me or frightened, but Squeak never showed up.

A week later, Mom went to play the organ. That's when we discovered Squeak had found a new home—that brand new, very expensive organ my dad bought for her. It didn't work because Squeak had chewed away all the wiring.

I was glad we found Squeak safe and happy. My mom wanted to kill him for what he'd done to her new organ.

"You can't hurt Squeak. He's family!" I pleaded.

"Okay, then I'll give him away!" she said. But it was an idle threat. Mom truly was a loving individual and Squeak went back in his cage, with plenty of his favorite peanut butter and honey. Funny thing, he never again chewed on his door when I played Glenn Miller. I think that hamster was making a statement.

Four Mischievous Brothers

Four mischievous brothers? Well, really only three older brothers. They were the mischievous ones.

My younger brother Ronny? He was my mischievous entertainment.

This started early: I loved putting ice cubes in Ronny's diaper. He had these cloth diapers with a big gap in the back at his waist. It was as if that diaper begged for an ice cube. Ronny would whine, cry and pull on the back of his diaper. By the time my mom changed him, she thought he was wet. I thought this was very funny. Now, I know it was mean, but siblings do stupid stuff to each other. We love each other to this day, and I took over as Ronny's pseudo mom when my father died and my mom became very busy.

But we were talking about mischief. Steve, my oldest brother, was always the instigator. I'm amazed that my other two big brothers weren't seriously hurt or killed implementing his crazy ideas. One of Steve's brilliant ideas was to build a three-story tree house forty feet in the air. He talked Ty, the youngest of my older brothers, into letting him tie a rope around his leg and swing the other end over an oak tree branch about fifteen feet in the air. Steve then secured that end of the rope to the back hitch on the garden tractor. The idea was that Steve could drive the tractor fast enough that Ty would be lifted up into the air, landing on the branch. Gary, the middle brother, was to signal to Steve when Ty reached the top of the tree.

Thank goodness my mother, while conducting bridge club, saw Ty hanging upside down in front of the picture window while Steve had the "pedal to the metal" on the garden tractor. Did they really think that Steve's idea was going to work? Was Ty likely to just fly through the air and land on the branch like an acrobat? He was barely coordinated enough to walk and run.

While they were building the treehouse, Steve and Gary had Ty hand them tools from the ground. When they were finished with the saw or hammer, they just tossed it back down. Should they have been surprised when they asked Ty to provide the next tool, and he didn't respond because he was lying flat on the ground knocked out by Steve's hammer?

Despite the tribulations, the tree house, when they finally finished it, was fantastic. It was three stories, with a rope swing hanging over it that reached a tree about fifty feet away. My brothers built a landing platform on it. We spent hours swinging back and forth. I would love to know who the fool was that climbed some forty feet to a top limb to tie that rope. Maybe the Blooming Prairie Fire Department helped? I wouldn't be surprised. That's how small towns function.

It's a wonder the Fire Department didn't have a station in our yard. My brothers were always up to something that risked limb, if not life. My mother tried her best to keep them out of trouble. Once, she insisted that my father build a gym in our basement. "These boys need a place to play and get rid of their extra energy," she said.

My father built a wonderful gym. It had water pipes that the boys could swing on, mattresses on the floor for soft landings and ropes dangling from the ceiling. There were also hammers and tools that the boys could use to entertain themselves. It was a safe place for young boys to play without supervision.

After a week of solitude and peace, my mother went down to the basement to give it a quick cleaning. She came running up and told my father, "You need to have Mr. Lysne come over and look at the foundation of the house. The boys aren't interested in the gym—they used the tools to chisel out the bricks so they could hide their toy guns behind them. I should've checked on them when they were being so quiet."

That basement went through many transitions. After it was a gym where we hung from the water pipes and performed gymnastic exercises, it became the local hangout, with a cool bar that my brother Ty built. Many parties started or ended there. Were my mom and dad aware of what was going on? Oh yeah, they were at work most of the time or maybe they were worn out and figured that at least they knew where we were.

I don't remember Mom playing bridge when I came along. I think my brothers put an end to it. The garden tractor incident was traumatic enough. But the time she looked out the window and saw her three boys peeing on the mint that she'd just put in the iced tea she was serving her guests was a warning that hosting bridge wasn't a great idea.

If she'd been smart, she would have quit after the tractor trailer incident. That day, my mom was hosting eleven ladies as bridge guests at our home on Main Street, kitty corner to the then Lutheran church. She had asked an older neighbor boy to watch Steve. Gary and Ty were content to play with their toys in the other room, but Steve, well, he had no fear and had to be tethered to a clothesline when he was little because he would just start walking and never look back.

The bridge game was active and my mother was trying to get the dessert and coffee ready when it was her turn to be the "bridge dummy". The neighbor boy came in from outside and kept trying to get my mother's attention.

"Just wait a minute. I'll get you boys some dessert when I get everyone served," she said.

"Mrs. Thorson, I need to talk to you." He began yanking on her skirt.

"Hold on. I know you want a snack. By the way, where's Steve?" she asked as she dished up Lemon Meringue Angel Pie.

"That's what I've been trying to tell you. We were playing on a tractor trailer with brand new John Deere tractors on the truck bed. Steve was having a blast pretending to drive one of the tractors on the semi-trailer bed. Well, the driver must have been napping and he woke up and started the truck. I jumped off, but Steve didn't. I guess I should've got him off the tractor because I know he's only five years old. Well, anyway, the truck is gone."

"What!" my mom yelled as she looked out of the front window to see the tractor trailer making a left turn heading for Highway 218.

She jumped into the car to follow the semi-truck, leaving the bridge club to fend for itself. The neighbor boy was in tow to keep an eye out for my brother.

When my mom caught up to the truck, Steve was having a heyday pretending to drive the tractor as it was moving.

Mom was terrified. She got in the other lane and pulled up even to his window, waving for the truck driver to pull over. He wasn't complying. There wasn't a place to pull over on Highway 218 without blocking the roadway. Finally, the neighbor boy rolled down his window and yelled that there was a boy sitting on a tractor on his trailer bed and he might die.

The driver slowed down and stopped. I guess he gave my mom an ear-full. He said he wasn't stopping for over two hundred miles and he shuddered to think of the possible consequences. I'm sure my poor mother gained a few grey hairs over that experience.

Three Legs Will Do

The first time my father and I really connected was over horses. A stately lawyer who worked in Blooming Prairie, Minnesota, my dad was tall, overweight and old enough to be my great grandfather (he was 64 when I was born), with a habit of chewing on his tongue when he was thinking or working. He owned two suits, both black. I recall him in those suits with a white shirt, no tie, and a belly that won the battle of the bulge over his belt. He went to work every day and saw his farmer clients into the wee hours of the night when they came out of the fields. Maybe that's why I have so few memories of him.

Or maybe it was because he had four sons and I was the only girl. He didn't seem to know how to interact with a daughter.

Whatever the reason, it wasn't surprising that my father wasn't involved when, at the age of three, I fell in love with horses. That was the first summer I remember going out to Northeast Montana to my Uncle Cal's farm on the Porcupine Creek, as I did every summer with my mother and brothers. My uncle had thousands of acres and a herd of horses. I was in my glory. Sitting for hours watching the foals play, riding through the woods collecting chokecherries, or helping out in the hay fields—that was my idea of fun. My father stayed home and worked. He wasn't a cowboy.

When I wasn't in Montana, I would watch *Roy Rogers, My Friend Flicka,* or *Fury* on our small black and white TV whenever it was my turn to choose a show from our choice of three channels. Horses were my passion. I entertained myself by pretending to be a horse. I did this for hours at a time, throwing my arms in the air, rearing, snorting through my nose, and softly blowing air out of my lips.

All I wanted to do was live in a barn and have a horse. I begged for a pony for my birthday and Christmas every year, and every year, my father told me all the reasons why I couldn't have one. I knew them by heart. "We live in town." "You're too young." "It costs too much money." "You don't know anything about caring for a horse." Blah, Blah, Blah. I had responses, but I'd learned early on that you couldn't argue with an attorney.

I consoled myself by riding my bike four miles to sneak into Mr. Oswald's pasture and ride his broodmare ponies. A piece of hay baling twine looped over the nose and another piece I used as reins gave me enough control so that I stayed on those unbroken ponies until I was scraped off by a low-hanging branch.

Mr. Oswald never knew I was riding his ponies until a pony rubbed me off on a tree. I got caught trying to catch her. I was terrified, but he was only worried for my safety. After this, Mr. Oswald and I pleaded with my father to buy me a pony.

At the age of eleven, I had the great idea to write a contract for a pony as my birthday present. After all, my father was a lawyer and my mother a paralegal. I'd been listening for years while the farmers sat at our dining room table discussing agricultural contracts. I used my mom's typewriter with a carbon copy and proceeded with all necessary agreements for purchasing and care of a pony at the time I turned thirteen. Then I presented the contract to my parents. My father smiled. My mother was impressed that I had actually acquired some legal skills. My dad signed it and wrote 'Oh, yeah' at the bottom of the document. I cut those two words off with scissors and waited.

My thirteenth birthday arrived and I went through all of the typical birthday hoopla. Girls from school were running around screaming and waving their hands with excitement to see all the Barbie and Ken dolls with cars and houses to match. I couldn't have cared less. I was waiting for the girls to go home. I had another agenda.

My father arrived home around eight that night and I met him at the door with my contract.

"This is ridiculous," he said when I handed it to him.

"You can't have a horse. We live in town. We've talked about this."

My mother chimed in. "Glenn that is a legal binding contract. You signed and dated it." She looked at me with admiration, impressed that I'd saved the piece of paper for two years.

"If you go down to paragraph four, you can read how I'll take care of my pony even in the dead of winter."

I was not backing down. I had a friend whose father was a farmer. I talked to her parents, who said they would exchange pasture board for my catching their piglets to put in the truck to take them to the market. Mr. Easton never thought the attorney's daughter would 'stoop so low' as to dodge the angry sow and run through pig manure to catch slippery piglets. Little did he know that my brothers routinely used me as a live target for their Dodge Ball practice and that I was strong from wrestling and racing up the swing-set poles with the neighbor boys. Besides, I couldn't think of anything I wouldn't do to have a horse of my own.

But would my dad concede? I pled my case as well as I could and I waited.

Coming home from school one day a week or so later, I found my dad was home early from work.

"Get in the car," he said. "We're going to get your pony."

"Really?" I couldn't believe it.

Dad didn't say a word the whole time he drove to Brownsdale. Maybe it was because I was doing most of the talking.

Pulling into a farm with a trailer house and a yard that was littered with old trucks, cars, used tires, rusted wire and containers, my father had to look hard to find a place to park. The grass hadn't been mowed and the implements looked like they hadn't worked in years.

"Sit in the car," he said. "I'll be back in a minute."

My dad went inside the trailer. I later learned he traded writing a will for my pony.

I did sit for a few minutes, but my enthusiasm was bursting at the seams. I looked out of the window and saw a cute black and white pony standing at a barbed wire fence that only came to her knees. Whoops, not knees, just knee. She had two legs in the back, but only one in the front. I got out of the car and pulled some clover to feed to her. She had the warmest expression and her eyes were soft and kind.

I stepped over the fence and played with her. She didn't seem to care as long as the handfuls of grass and clover kept coming. Then I waved my hands to get her to move. She cantered in an unusual way, but she was quick and looked sturdy. Walking over to the barn, I found a piece of baling twine and made a loop to fit over her muzzle. I tied another piece of twine into a pair of reins and hopped on her back. She burst forward and scooted around while I hung on for dear life, but eventually she settled down and I was able to get her to walk on command. She was sweet and I was bonding with her. She could canter, but there wasn't a trot. I could live with that.

I hopped off and removed the twine just before my dad and Mr. Johnson came out. I ran back to the car and stood by the door. My dad and the owner walked up.

"I'll take her. What's her name?" I said as I pointed and turned to look at my new three-legged pony.

I heard coughing and spitting and turned around. My father and Mr. Johnson were laughing hysterically. Dad was laughing so hard that he had to walk over to a fence post to hold himself up. I had never seen him like that.

"Her name is Solo," Mr. Johnson managed to say. She caught her leg in an old plow in the pasture and we use her for a broodmare. She isn't broke to ride."

He could hardly contain himself. "Glenn, if I'd known that your daughter had such a great sense of humor, I wouldn't have made you take out the time to write my will in exchange for the cost of a pony. The laugh was worth the price."

Mr. Johnson walked over to the barn and pulled out a fourteen-hand brown and white pinto with a little western saddle and bridle.

"Sweetie, this is your pony," he said, handing me the reins.

I never told them that I rode the three-legged pony. I just hopped on the pinto, my new pony, and cantered her down the road. I had no fear and the pony must have sensed that. She spooked at some birds that flew out of the field. Stopping her was a little difficult, but I decided to ride her the eight miles to her new barn, worried that my dad might change his mind.

When I didn't return to the Johnson's barn, my father began to get worried. He drove to our house, and my mother knew right away where I would head. She suggested they drive out to the farm where I was going to keep the pony.

To this day, I'm not sure if my parents realized the risk of a young girl riding a new pony next to a highway or if they had the confidence I could manage it. I prefer to believe the latter.

I bedded down my pony in her new stall with a small pail of grain, bucket of water, a flake of hay and an apple I had stowed away in my coat pocket. I was hungry, but it was more important for me to feed that apple to my new pony.

Then I saw my mother and father drive up in the car. My dad had an angry look on his face. "I waited for you at Mr. Johnson's barn. Why didn't you come back?"

"I didn't want to take the risk that you would change your mind. Too late now," I said.

My mother was hiding the smile on her face. My father softened and then asked, "What are you going to name her?"

"Lady. She didn't bite, kick, buck or rub me off on a branch. She's sweet."

Shortly after my thirteenth birthday, my father became quite ill with diabetes and cancer, but that didn't stop him from helping me in the middle of the night one time. Little did we know that my new pony was pregnant and so we got two equines for one price.

I had tethered my pony to a chain with a stake in our back yard so I could ride her early in the morning. I woke up after midnight to the sound of her whinnying. I waited awhile and she didn't stop.

I went outside and was shocked to see a leg sticking out from her behind. Panicking, I woke up my dad. Though he was old and in pain, he tried to pull the colt out with his bare hands. But the baby was stuck.

We called the veterinarian, Mr. Magnusson, but he was out delivering calves and couldn't help. It was a critical situation. We could tell my pony was going into shock and she was in danger of dying.

My dad wrapped the colt's two legs that were both sticking out with a towel and wrapped a rope around the towel, then tying the other end of the rope to the garden tractor hitch. He instructed me to stay with Lady. I knew how to turn the legs and adjust the head on the baby because I used to ride along and help Mr. Magnusson deliver calves. He slowly made the rope taut and it was enough pressure to pull the baby out. The tractor, and my adjusting, saved Lady and her colt. My Dad was my hero.

Dad died a few years later. I've always been grateful that we bonded with the help of that pony and I can still see him laughing and hanging on to that fence post as if it happened yesterday.

Mom's Mishaps

I had two children. I couldn't imagine having five. Especially the three oldest boys that were only four-years apart. When we were adults, my mother, Isabelle, talked about her child-rearing days fondly, and I know she had a few tricks up her sleeve to help her cope. For one, she filled the sandbox with a vast number of toys. By the time they were used by my youngest brother, those metal bulldozers, cranes and dump trucks had seen better days.

It was early December in Blooming Prairie, Minnesota, and my mom was preparing for the holidays. Feeding a family of seven required an extensive grocery list. As usual, Mom was juggling tasks; answering the phone for clients from the law office, overseeing my writing of a high school research paper, jotting down the grocery list, trying to figure out who would get what for Christmas and tackling a refurbishing project.

"Mom what are you doing to Ronny's sandbox toys?" I asked. "Are you going to have time to type my paper for Mr. Sheldon's history class project? I can't believe we had to put all the information on three by five cards and write down all our sources. I don't get it. If it's already written down, why do we need to write it down again? I think history is stupid. I live for today," I said, trying to rationalize—and prepare my mother—why my final grade would be marginal at best.

"It makes you think and it teaches you how to do research. Yes, I'll get to it while I wait for the paint on the toys to dry."

"Dry? What are you going to do to them? They're kind of yucky."

"I'm taking the wheels off and spray painting them black, and then spray painting the chassis red. Then I'm going to wrap them up and give them to Ronny for Christmas. He'll think they're new. Then they'll go back to the sandbox to rust again," she said with great pride.

"Really? What are you repairing of mine to give me for Christmas?"

"I'm doing this only for the sandbox toys. It's ridiculous to buy something new that will just rust outside."

"Mom, there's a new product out. It's called plastic and it doesn't rust."

"Those plastic toys just break and they don't last. These trucks have lasted decades."

"I'll have to admit, you do like antiques. You and dad are the most frugal people I know."

We didn't have a clothes dryer. My blue jeans were stuck in a ninety degree angle after drying on the radiators. Oh, and Dad! He finally had to get another used car when the only gear he had was reverse. He would have kept the car if he could have figured out what side of the road he could drive on. We were the last family in town to get a phone and a TV. We still didn't have a color TV. It was heavenly to see Disneyland and the Peacock in color. I loved it when the Hanson's needed a babysitter. They had a color TV and a pool table. Neat stuff.

"It builds character to struggle and I'm teaching you to be happy with what you have," my mom said, giving me the 'parent look'.

"Okay, I get it. It looks like you need help with the painting. I'll spread out newspapers and hose off the sand first."

"That'll be great. I'm just finishing the grocery list that I'm sending with your dad and then I'll get the spray paint ready. By the way, how much Jell-O should I order? Are six boxes of family size enough?"

"I think you should get a dozen. The way you go through Jell-O recipes and with everyone home for

Christmas, it's a staple around here. Let's see, Jell-O with mandarin oranges, Jell-O with cool whip, Jell-O with fruit cocktail, Jell-O with orange juice and ginger ale, Jell-O with marshmallows, Jell-O…"

"Okay, stop. That's enough. I'll get one dozen family size." She quickly made the correction.

"I'm going to be at the house finishing up some estates, painting these toys and then typing Kathy's research paper," she told my dad as he was headed out the door. "I'll be into work after that. Here's the grocery list for Betlach's Grocery. They're going to deliver." She handed the list to my father.

"Don't be too long," he said. "Clients prefer to talk to you. They like their bad information sugar-coated. I'm not good at that."

"Great. Got that done. Now on to Ronny's toys."

"I rinsed the sand off, but the compacted dirt didn't come out of the inside," I said, trying to pry it out with a knife from the silver ware drawer.

"Don't use that knife. No wonder I can't seem to keep silverware."

Meanwhile, with much effort, Mom was able to get the wheels off and the chassis separated to be sprayed fire-engine red. Ronny was almost nine years old and I figured he would know these weren't new, but then again, it was the surprise of opening the presents that counted.

After Mom sprayed the truck bodies, they looked rather nice. She was pulling this off and I was impressed.

"I see that Betlach's grocery truck is here. Tell them to go around back to drop off the groceries," Mom instructed. "I'm having a little problem with the black spray paint jamming and the color's not coming out."

I went out to meet the delivery boy.

"Your mom must be entertaining a bunch of people. The National Guard is coming to town. Does your mom have something planned?" he asked.

"Not that I know of. But then again, I'm the last one to know what goes on here. Mom wants you to use the back door to drop off the groceries."

"No problem. It'll take a little while."

I went back to Mom's project. She was using a pin to open up the nozzle of the black spray paint can. It kept getting plugged, but she only had a couple of wheels left. We both noticed, as we intermittently looked out the kitchen window, that the delivery boy was going back and forth to the back door over and over again.

"What's he doing? Is he carrying one tiny bag or box at a time?" Mom asked.

"I don't know. He asked if we were going to be entertaining the National Guard."

"What stories will they come up with next?" Mom said laughing.

The delivery boy poked his head in the door and said, "We didn't have enough family-sized Jell-O so we gave you two regular size for each family size."

Just then the black spray can began to spray, hitting my mother in the face. She dropped the can and it began spraying the kitchen, the furniture and everything else in its way. It was jammed open.

The grocery boy took one look and bolted off to his delivery truck. This mess was more than he could handle. I was trying to grab the spray paint can, but it was spinning out of control, and it was slippery. By the time the can ran out of paint and finally stopped on its own, Mom and I were completely covered in black paint.

"Oh, my. Look at this place. It's a mess. How are we going to get that black paint off of everything?" I asked in horror. I couldn't believe how bad my mom looked. Her face was black with two white spots where her eyes squinted shut. Her hair was normally light brown, but now she had a new hairdo. Light brown with black matted streaks. *She'll have to shave it!* Then there were her arms, hands, legs (yes, the nylons didn't spare her) and her fingers. Her typing fingers. *OH, NO! Who's going to type my paper?*

"Mom, how are we going to clean you up?"

"There's some paint thinner in the back hallway. Go get it and hurry," she said as she was trying to wipe black paint off with a towel.

I tried to push open the swinging door to the back hallway, but it wouldn't budge.

"Somethings blocking the door," I said. "I'll go around to the back door."

When I entered our back room after braving the frigid Minnesota air, I couldn't believe it. The room looked like a grocery warehouse. Boxes were stacked on top of each other. There must have been twenty or thirty large cardboard boxes that said Jell-O. I knew mom was busy, but I thought she needed to see this. Plus, there was no way I was going to be able to get to the closet with the paint thinner. I went back around to the front door and into the kitchen.

"Mom, we have a problem. The back of the house is filled with boxes and I think they're mostly Jell-O. That's why we can't open the swinging door."

"What? You must be confused." She tried to open the door to the back of the house herself.

"You have to go outside and around the back and its cold out," I said as I followed her.

The look on her face when she walked in through the back door was priceless. "There must be a major mistake. This isn't my order. I better call the grocery store."

"You can't. The boxes are blocking the way to the phone."

"I'll just get in the car and go down there. Oh, that's right. Your dad took the car."

"I'm glad he did, Mom. Have you looked at yourself in the mirror? I don't think you should go downtown. And what about my paper?" I asked.

Mom got a glimpse of herself in the mirror over the back hall sink.

"Oh, my, this won't do. I won't be going to work today. Well, after I wash my hands, I'll type your paper."

That was my mom. Still living up to her commitment even in the midst of adversity. I later learned that my mom, when she looked at the grocery list, realized she had added the number *one* without erasing the *six*, and then added a *dozen* in front of the words *family size Jell-O*. She'd ordered sixteen dozen family-size boxes of Jell-O when she meant to order six. And the grocery store gave her two regular boxes of Jell-O for every family size because they ran out of family size Jell-O It's rare for a grocery store to run out of family-sized Jell-O in Minnesota. We had over 330 boxes of Jell-O. Fortunately, the store took back the extra boxes. I never did see that delivery boy again.

And Mom's new look? Well, it took a while for the black to fade, but Ag Shafer, the local hairdresser, was able to do wonders with her hair.

Attending College in Mankato

Car Troubles

My first car was a 1960 Valiant that I bought from my brother Steve. It had a screwdriver for a stick shift and there was only one seat in the car—the driver's seat.

I didn't care. It would get me from point A to point B. That was all that mattered to me. Seat belts weren't required—and besides, with no seats, where would I put them?—so I could pile a lot of kids in the car.

The Valiant was a frog-green color and it had no muffler, so it was no secret when I came or went. It didn't last long because Steve borrowed it one night and left it parked on a hill. It rolled into a pond because it didn't have a parking brake.

He wasn't about to claim it. It was okay, because then he sold me his 1966 Burgundy Toronado. Wow, was that a beast. I looked like an ant behind the steering wheel, but I could cruise a hundred miles an hour.

One time I drove home from Mankato to Blooming Prairie in about half the time it was supposed to take so I would make it to my job, teaching swimming lessons and life guarding at the pool next to my house. After I stopped the car in front of the gate to the pool, I hopped out and started unlocking the gate to let the children in for their swimming lesson.

I heard a grinding and whining sound and noticed that the kids' parents were looking at my car. In fact, everyone was looking at my car, but me.

All of a sudden the hood blew open and the radiator spewed water about ten feet in the air. I just shrugged and headed down to the pool to work. Since I knew nothing about cars and motors. I figured this was no big deal. It turned out all I needed to do was put some more water in the radiator.

I loved that car. However, my insurance company didn't. I acquired thirteen speeding tickets in one year. *Not good.*

I remember the last time I met Judge Cashman in the Steel county courtroom for speeding. I had a ticket for thirty-five-miles-an hour over the designated speed limit of fifty-five.

It was okay. I had a story. Or should I say, I had a lie.

Harrison Oswald, the man whose ponies I use to ride, was also in the courtroom for a speeding ticket. I sat next to him and I told him how I was going to get out of the ticket. I had made up a story. I told the highway patrol man about how my boyfriend was in the hospital and that was why I was speeding—I needed to get to the hospital.

The patrolman was very sympathetic and let me go to court so I could explain it to the judge and have the ticket dismissed.

Mr. Harrison was impressed. I also told him how I escaped the other twelve tickets. I guess a smile and pleading ignorance worked for me back then. It doesn't now.

My name was called and I gave Mr. Oswald a confident smile as I walked up to the bench.

"How would you like to plead, Miss Thorson?" Judge Cashman asked.

"Not guilty," I said as I stood up as straight as I could.

"Could you plead your case, please?" the judge said.

This was the chance for my dramatic skills to kick in. I took a deep breath and, with a doe-eyed look designed to create the most sympathy possible, I pled away "I received a phone call that my boyfriend had been in a terrible accident. It was all I could do, just get in my car and drive as fast as I could to Mankato. I was crying and praying the whole way. It was just pitiful. I was so worried and so in love."

I looked around. Judging from the looks of the other people in the courtroom, my plea seemed to have gone well.

Mr. Harrison smiled and nodded approvingly. "Really? Is that right, Miss Thorson? Well, I had my assistants read the state trooper's report and they checked all the hospitals and doctor's offices and even called the family of your said boyfriend. There was no accident or hospitalization reported."

"Would you like to change your plea, Miss Thorson?" Judge Cashman said with a stern look on his face.

I was mortified. The courtroom broke into laughter. Mr. Oswald was laughing the loudest.

Judge Cashman hit his gravel on the bench and I could tell he was even angrier.

"Oh. Really? Wow, I guess I'm guilty. Sorry, I didn't tell the truth," I said as I lowered my head.

"Let me tell you something, young lady. I know your father and he would be appalled by your behavior."

"Do you know why we have speed limits? It's to protect you and others. I've checked your speeding record and I want you to know that if I ever see you in this courtroom again, I'll take your license away for the rest of your life. Is that what you want?" He was leaning over his bench and staring me directly in the face.

Tears streamed down my face. He made his point and it was a lesson I have never forgotten. Especially since it came back to haunt me.

Years later, not long after I married my husband, Bill, he came home upset one day after work.

"What's wrong?" I asked when I saw the look on his face.

"I got a speeding ticket for ten miles over on my way to the hospital and the insurance company cancelled our policy. I know we can't afford a premium hike."

"Ten miles over? That's chicken feed! They can't do that," I said. "Listen. I know. I'm an attorney's daughter. You go back to the insurance office at the Mayo Clinic and you give them hell. That's not right and they will reinstate our insurance."

He was beaming with confidence as he went out the door.

A couple of hours later, my husband came back home. I hardly recognized him. His eyes and mouth were distorted. They were just slits. Where was his usual mild expression?

"Well, what happened?" I asked.

He threw a piece of paper on the table. "It wasn't my speeding ticket that caused the problem. It was your thirteen.

"When you're married they combine your records for insurance? Oh, that's wrong."

Needless to say, it was an expensive three years of high-risk insurance premiums. I had to take a couple of extracurricular coaching positions at the high school in order to cover the price of the new policy.

Did I say coaching? Oh, yes, I was the head volleyball coach and I'd never played volleyball in my life. But that's another true story.

"Blind" Denise Tour

My college years were one big experiment. Money was scarce, but creativity was abundant. I learned how to make an idea work and how people communicated. My major was in the field of communication disorders and I loved being a speech pathologist. Since I wanted to work with special needs children, I volunteered at many schools, clinics and hospitals, learning how handicaps impacted a person's life. It was such a rewarding job.

One volunteer job in which I spent many hours, was reading to the blind students at my university. I also learned how to walk with them when they wanted to leave their apartment, and what they thought about their future and their fears. I was amazed that many of them didn't have an issue with fear. They were confident and strong despite their disability.

I couldn't imagine. Of course, sometimes I would make faux pas during our conversations, like, "Did you watch the movie about……?" "You need to see the new art exhibit….." "I can't wait to show you……" "Oh my, look at that guy, he's gorgeous," and on and on. Usually I'd stand corrected when I heard giggles or would stop when they shook their heads. I learned to come back with a funny comment to make them laugh, which was so much better than an awkward silence. Often I would apologize by saying, "Sorry, that was a dumb thing to say. I didn't just put my foot in my mouth. I inserted my whole leg."

At the time, I was living in an apartment with a group of girls that I'm friends with to this day. It was like having seven sisters—a new experience for me since I grew up with four brothers in a neighborhood of mostly boys.

It was a female social experiment. The greatest difference between girls and boys at that age is how they fight. When there was an argument, girls don't grab you around the neck and do "hot potato" on your head. Or wrestle you to the ground and sit on your chest with a wad of spit slowly dripping from their mouth to land between your eyes. No. Women are sneaky and definitely able to win verbally. It was a skill that I learned and it became invaluable.

One of the girls, Denise, had a cabin in northern Minnesota that was about a six-hour drive away. We had a blast taking her family's speed boat out on the lake, visiting the local venues, and just getting crazy. It was the early 70s and life was wild. The Vietnam War was raging, free love was around every corner, pot was grown in backyards and I'm sure our parents thought the world was going to hell.

We lived on cash. There were no credit cards or ATMs. I wrote letters to every Vietnam veteran that I knew who was fighting for our country that was drafted from my hometown. It was the least I could do. I'm friends with those people to this day, also.

One trip my roommates, The Tunas, took to Denise's cabin was quite memorable. After minimum sleep, specialty drinks and sore abdominal muscles from laughing too hard, it was time to head home. We'd spent most of our money and there was nothing left to do. Denise was riding with me and it was just the two of us in the car.

The story goes like this:

"Denise, we're going to run out of gas. Do you have any money?"

"I have a couple of dollars. How about you?"

"I have a couple of dollars, too. We'll stop at the next gas station and hopefully we'll have enough to get home. We can drive slowly to conserve gas," I said, not sure that was possible since I had a lead foot.

As we were heading down the local two-lane road to Mankato, Minnesota, after getting our gas, I saw a billboard advertising a Native American Museum. (In those days, every billboard offered new and more exciting discoveries.)

"Denise, have you been seeing these billboards advertising this museum? It must be huge. Like Disneyland or something. I bet I've seen at least five of them," I said.

"Did you see what it cost?" she said. "We don't have any money left after filling the car."

"I'm sure there are shops and stuff that we can walk around for free. Let's go."

We took the exit for the museum and traveled down a one-lane road for miles. I was wondering if we would have enough gas to make it home. Just when I thought seriously about turning around, there it was. A tiny, Native American village surrounded by a six-foot fence with a person sitting at a ticket booth.

The sign read:

Adults $5.00
Children $2.00
Students and Teachers Free

"Oh no, we don't have any money. I can't believe we wasted our time and gas," Denise said.

"I have an idea. I worked with the blind at school. I'll be the teacher and you be the blind student and we'll get in free," I said. "I promise it'll work."

"Are you sure? How are we going to pull this off?"

"I'll fix you up. Put on your sunglasses and I'm going to clean a branch from a tree for you to use as a walking stick. I'm going to hold your arm and tell you what to do for every step.

"Don't worry. I got this," I said proudly as I headed for the tree with the easiest branches to clean.

"You swing the stick back and forth on the ground like this," I added, after handing her the cleaned tree limb.

We approached the ticket booth.

I took the lead. "Hello, we drove many miles to come to see your museum because of the fact that students and teachers are free. How wonderful that you offer this service," I said, hoping my schmoozing would help.

"Where are your students? I don't see a bus and I wasn't called in advance." Clearly, the ticket person was suspicious.

"I'm the teacher and this is my student, Denise. She's blind. We have traveled a long way. A very long way."

"How is she going to see the exhibits? We don't have any audio programs to accommodate the blind," she said.

"No problem. That's what I'm here for," I said, not looking at Denise for fear we would start laughing.

"Okay. Next time call and make arrangements. Here are your tickets."

We were in and we both started giggling as we looked at each other. Denise was very good at swinging her stick and I told her everywhere to go and when to step up if the ground was uneven. I think we convinced ourselves that this experience was real.

We arrived at the first teepee and went inside. It was quite large and there was a small group of people inside with a guide describing the artifacts.

We sat in the back. A person came in and whispered to the guide. The next thing I knew, the man was heading in our direction.

"We have a special guest today and I'm going to give her an experience that I'm sorry all of you can't share."

He stood in front of us and he grabbed Denise's arm. "This girl is blind and so I'm going to let her touch and feel the artifacts that I'm describing."

He whisked Denise away before I could get a word in. She turned to me and the words she mouthed can't be printed in this story, but I did get the gist, which was that I'd better get her out of this predicament.

Meanwhile, he took her to the front of the room and began describing how the Indians created maps out of fur. Having her hand forced to touch the hundred-year-old hide wasn't something Denise was finding enjoyable. She kept turning her head and giving me the evil eye. Not that I could see it through her sunglasses, but I'd seen that look on her face before.

Next it was the pottery, then the arrowheads, the tomahawks, the bones. Lots of them. I could tell that Denise was getting more and more irritated. On top of this, we were a long way from home. If I let her continue in this situation, the trip would take even longer.

I had to save her, but I was also enjoying the history lesson. How was I going to pull off a rescue without exposing our fraud?

Then I had an idea. I went up to the instructor and told him that Denise needed a bathroom break. I was sure she wanted to wash her hands.

When we got to the bathroom, Denise let me have it.

"I can't believe I had to touch that stuff. It was gross. This was your stupid idea and I'm the hell out of here." She threw the stick in the garbage, pushed her sunglasses on top of her head and headed for the door.

"Wait! I have to walk you out of here."

"You aren't walking me anywhere. I'm going home."

She went out the door, and there was the guide. "We waited for you so we can go into more history about how the natives prepared meals," he said.

Denise took one look at him and began running for the entrance. No stick and no sunglasses.

"She's healed. She can see. It's a miracle!" I said as I went running after her trying to contain my laughter.

We made it to the car, but the looks we received from the guide, the ticket taker, and other spectators were priceless.

I'm sure I'll have to pay my penance for being untruthful, but it was an experience neither Denise nor I will ever forget.

Montana Madness

Friends and adventure seem to go hand in hand, especially when you are in college and free. What would be more fun than to go to Glacier National Park driving a 1966 Toronado pulling a homemade Teardrop Camper?

My car was only six years old at the time and I'm not sure that's the name of the camper today, so I'll describe it. Fancy it wasn't, but functional it was. It was shaped like a sideways teardrop, with two small tires the size of a large lawn mower.

This didn't put a damper on my idea of camping in luxury: It held a king-size bed (that would easily sleep three girls), cabinets on one side (that would easily hold wadded up shirts and pants), and two small doors with windows (that reduced claustrophobia), along with a 'hood' in the very back that you lifted for access to the kitchenette.

It was perfect. It cost me $150, along with me promising a date which never happened.

My burgundy beast, the 1966 Toronado, was still going strong. It was something else, with its souped-up, V-8 engine that appeared to be longer than the rest of the car. I still had to put a pillow on the seat so I could look over the steering wheel, and it could still cruise at a hundred miles an hour, though maybe not while pulling a camper.

I asked two of my roommates, Denise and Beetie, if they wanted to brave a trip to Montana and Colorado the first week of June. I informed them that it would be the cheapest trip of all time. Staying with my cousins in Montana and in the camper while we were at the park was a budget a trio of poor college students could afford. They were on it like a fly on dung!

So, with a limited amount of cash, no credit card and no sense, we were on our way and up for a good time. We left Blooming Prairie with one map of the Midwest and maybe a pencil or two. We figured we could always ask for directions at a gas station. It was the 70s and we were girls after all. After packing plenty of beer (we were *close* to being twenty-one), Boones Farm Wine, bread, peanut butter and munchies, we were ready and on our way!

I think we drove straight through from Minnesota to Montana, but I don't know for sure. We could've stopped at the Badlands in North Dakota, but I'm terrified of rattlesnakes and think I voted against it. Then again, much of this vacation was in a state of altered consciousness so my memory this many years later could be skewed.

We landed in Nashua, Montana, at my Uncle Cal's farm mid-afternoon. We greeted my aunt, uncle and cousins with the normal hugs and kisses. They couldn't wait to show us around.

I couldn't believe it. They had built a brand new house. I loved the old farmhouse. I missed the water pump and a bathtub located outside in the back of what was basically a tarpaper shack. I remember watching my cousins heat water on a stove and poor it in the tub. Girls first—and I was always the first one to take a bath. The boys went after me. It made me feel special. The water was pretty grimy by the time the last boy (depending on whose family was there, it could be as many as five or six) had bathed.

Then my Uncle Cal motioned for me to go outside and see his brand-new pickup truck.

"There's time before we eat. Take it for a spin and show your friends Porky Pine Creek," Cal said.

Beetie, Denise, and I, along with a knapsack containing the beer and wine, hopped in and headed down the half-mile dirt road to party before dinnertime. I was experienced in removing the barbwire gate to the cow pasture at the top of the steep hill because I spent many summers there as a young girl, and in my early teens.

The wide open spaces, driving the hay truck, picking chokecherries and riding the horses was heaven. That was what Cal and I had in common—he loved riding, too. He was now a farmer, but he had ridden broncs in the rodeo. Cal looked like one of the cowboys in the Westerns that I watched on TV. Now the farm had a new, modern house. My uncle didn't need to ride a horse anymore. He had young hands to do that. So the horses were gone, though there were still many cows left on that thousand acres.

After Denise, Beetie and I went through the gate, I had to carefully descend the steep hill that had deep ditches on each side. I knew these roads, but the girls were a little queasy. I felt a twinge when we passed the dilapidated barn and broken-down corral. I'd enticed many horses into that small corral with grain so I could ride and round up the calves for the cowboys to castrate. The guys would throw the testicles at me and tell me to fry them up.

"No way, I'll stick to the jams and jellies," I'd say, not looking at the farm dogs that were fighting for the goodies.

We arrived at Porky Pine creek and it hadn't changed a bit. I saw the old swimming hole with the remnants of a pulley that hung from a tree that leaned over the creek which offered the chance to swing on a rope and land in the water.

I never saw a rattlesnake, but there seemed to be a rat snake around every corner. They were harmless and sometimes I would catch one to torment my cousins.

We were looking for the perfect spot to have our liquid picnic. The side of the creek we were driving on was too sunny and there weren't many trees. Then we saw it. There, across the creek, was a picnic spot to die for.

"I'm going to drive over there so we don't have to get wet," I told the girls.

I knew this creek and I remembered the crossing. Or so I thought. It had been almost eight years since I'd ridden along it. I think my judgement was slightly altered, also. I had been drinking the wine and the other girls were drinking the beer.

I got out of the truck and checked the bottom of the creek. The smooth stones that lined the creek bed seemed solid to me. I stomped on them and there wasn't any mud, so I felt safe to take my uncle's brand new truck across.

But halfway across the creek, the truck dropped in a hole. Water was flowing across the running board and into the truck. Obscenities were flying out of my mouth as Beetie and Denise started laughing.

The truck was buried up to the axle and I was hoping that it would stay put long enough for me to get help. I told the girls to keep an eye on it and I took off for the farmhouse on foot running as fast as I could.

I was dreading the steep hill. When I turned the corner by the old barn and corral, there in front of me was a horse. I couldn't believe my eyes. A gift from heaven. Uncle Cal must have kept at least one out of the herd. He did have a soft spot for horses.

I went into the barn and found an old rusty pail and a tattered bridle. I put some gravel in the bucket and began to shake it. The horse perked up and hesitantly followed me into the corral. I quickly took one of the rotten boards and wedged it between the posts where the gate used to be. When the horse realized he had been fooled and was trapped, he began to run clockwise around the corral looking for an escape route. I ran along side of him until I was able to swing the reins around his neck. I dug my heels into the ground and pulled him to a stop.

"Get me up that hill and to the farm and I'll give you an apple. Promise," I said in a calm voice.

I was able to bridle him and pulled him over to the side of the coral as I crawled up the weathered boards. He was very hesitant and head shy. I leaped on him bareback and off he went. He was at high speed and he broke right through the board I'd rigged up for a gate.

We were off to the races. I didn't care. He was running up that hill as fast as he could and I was hanging on for all I was worth. As I reached the top, my uncle's old Lincoln Continental was slowly leaving the gate.

I rode the horse up to his car and circled it at a gallop. The horse didn't have any steering or brakes. I had to drop one rein and pull the other to my knee to get the horse to turn.

"Where'd you get that horse and where's my truck?" Cal yelled from the open window.

"And where have you been? Dinner has been ready for an hour. We came looking for you," my aunt called from the passenger seat.

"This isn't your horse?" I said as I continued to circle the car as if I was in an old Western wagon train that was fighting off the Indians.

"Hell no, never seen it before. Doesn't look broke to me. Maybe the Tahistas bought him at the sale barn and put him in my pasture.

"Where's my truck?" he asked again.

"It's in the creek and we need the tractor to get it out," I yelled back.

I can't write the words that my uncle used. Not that I don't remember them, I just might not get the vulgarities in the right order. But I do remember him saying, "Get off that damn horse and get in the car."

At that point in time, I thought I was safer on the horse, but I didn't want to cross my uncle. I jumped off the horse and he stood still long enough for me to pull off the bridle. I've never seen a horse run away so fast.

I didn't say a word and neither did my aunt as my uncle drove like a maniac to the farmhouse. We both looked out the window as my uncle muttered to himself.

The road seemed longer than I had remembered. Cal jumped out of the car while it was still running and headed to the tractor shed. As my aunt went into the house, she told me to drive the car down to the creek and to be careful. "I'm calling Uncle Ronny to come help," she yelled.

I followed my uncle in the car as he drove the tractor in high gear to Porky Pine Creek. As we arrived, he looked at the empty beer cans and the wine bottle next to Denise and Beetie. I stopped the car and ran to the truck. Soon my other uncle appeared and between the two of them, they were able to pull the truck out. It was a mess, but was able to be driven.

"I'll clean it so it looks like new," I said.

"The hell you will. You aren't getting near this truck ever again," Cal said. I saw Beetie and Denise bite their lips so they wouldn't laugh.

We ate and stayed the night. The next morning, my uncle had one of his hired hands clean the truck. It cleaned up very nicely, but it had lost that 'new' smell. It was now slightly fishy. I think my aunt and uncle were a little relieved when we left that afternoon. He never mentioned the beer and wine. I was grateful for that.

As we headed west on highway US2 to Glacier Park, I told the girls about the horse that appeared right when I needed him. They didn't ever see him and I'm not sure they believed me. Every so often, one of us would burst out laughing and we didn't have to tell anyone what was so funny. We already knew.

We arrived at the park listening to the Moody Blues singing "Nights in White Satin." The snow peaks and pine trees were a beautiful sight for a bunch of flat-landers from Minnesota.

It turned out that we were too early in the season and the park wasn't open. The gate wasn't locked, so I opened it and we went ahead in. This was the early 70s and times were different: it was enter at your own risk.

It was getting dark and we were hungry. We managed to find a small campground and were the only ones there. I was looking forward to using my kitchenette and making s'mores over a small fire. After we ate, we decided to go to bed. It had been a long day.

In the middle of the night, I felt the back of the camper rock and move. Denise and Beetie were fast asleep. I looked out of the window and there was a bear. Obviously, he or she wanted to try out my kitchenette, too.

"Bear, Bear!" I yelled, but when the girls looked out the window, there was no bear.

"Are you sure?" Denise asked, half asleep.

"Yes, we have to get out of here. This camper is like a tin can." I grabbed the keys, and, when I didn't see the bear, jumped out of the trailer and into the car. I drove down the road a ways until I thought we were safe. It was a short park visit.

Then we were on our way to Colorado to visit our girlfriends Plunky and Ann. I stopped to get gas in Polson, Montana, and the gas station attendant looked at my car. There were small metal balls rolling out from behind my wheel.

"You can't drive this car," he said. "That's your ball bearings that's rolling down the drive. Your wheel will fall off. Sure lucky you weren't in the mountains."

"Can you fix it?" I asked.

"Nope, you're in the middle of nowhere. I can see if George has a car he could sell you. The closest city is a day's drive away," he said.

He called George and he had a Burgundy 1969 Chevy Impala. The color was the same, but the car was a step down in my opinion. My father had to wire the $600 for the car. We were able to use the hitch to attach the trailer. I was sad to leave my 1966 Toronado. It had served me well, except for the thirteen speeding tickets on my record.

Turning Twenty-One at Beaver Lake

I'm sure most people remember the what, who and where, when they turned twenty-one. I know I do.

If you don't, that's okay. As my father would say, "Some were born to work and some were born to enjoy it." He would point at me and say," You just happen to be in the first group." He didn't live long enough to see me turn twenty-one, when I moved to the second group. Maybe I couldn't be a member for long, but at least on my 21st birthday, I felt I was born to play.

The day started out rather boring. At the time, I was working for Jim Mork, the attorney that inherited my dad's law practice. I think he hired me out of pity, because I lost my job on the heels of losing my dad. I wasn't much of a secretary. He found that out quickly. Shorthand? Filing? Affidavits? No, not for me, but I could type and run errands.

I was supposed to run the pool, a summer job I had for five years, but it didn't work out. My dad had built the swimming pool and he had given it to the city, but the day after he died, I was fired—the new manager needed a job for his son. I was out and he was in.

It's okay that I was fired from the pool. I learned a lot about the legal system working in my mother's law office and that has helped me to this day. I never did teach swimming lessons or lifeguard again. That was okay, too. Jim Mork was a good guy. He couldn't help it that my 21st birthday started out boring typing contracts.

Besides, I knew the day was going to get better. My boyfriend had called a few days earlier and told me he had a surprise for my birthday. I rushed home from work to get ready. I had bought a new dress, makeup and shoes for the occasion. I was ready to go out on the town and be able to order a drink legally—it was a rite of passage.

My boyfriend showed up in a pair of old blue jeans, holding a paper bag with raw pork chops and a bottle of cheap wine. I was dressed to the nines. Awkward!

"I thought we could cook these pork chops on the grill and drink this bottle of wine," he said.

"We aren't going out?" I asked. "This is my 21st birthday."

"No, I had to fix my MG, so I'm a little short of money."

Yes, the MG he tinkered with incessantly and worshipped even more incessantly. I hated that car. We always took mine when we needed to go anywhere.

No worries, though, the birthday story doesn't end here. After the meal, I told him that I didn't feel well (I don't eat pork because it doesn't agree with me) and I was calling it a night. He went home and I changed into my robe. Then I got pissed. That triggered one of my most sacred mantras: *When angry, call your girlfriends.*

"I'm on my way to pick you up!" I said to Penny, Denise and Beetie, "I want to go into a bar and order a drink legally." Not that I'm a big drinker. That wasn't the point. I wanted to feel like an adult, a big person with rights.

So, we did just that. We went barhopping to Austin, Minnesota, and went into every bar that was appropriate. No meat markets. Austin was a happening place before the Hormel Plant had a run-in with their union workers which was produced into a documentary.

Penny, Denise, Beetie and I finished up at a bar in Geneva. I was feeling no pain by then and it was time for my designated drivers to take me home.

The story might have ended here. But then we passed Beaver Lake. I screamed, "Pull over!"

I jumped out of the car and ran to the beach. That "no pain" I was feeling was accompanied by "no inhibition." I stripped off my clothes and swam out to the dock. It was around midnight, so there were no lights and no one around.

Penny and Denise, when they realized they couldn't stop me, thought they better swim out with me to make sure I would be okay. So they disrobed, too. Beetie stayed with the car.

I was doing dives off the high board on the dock: one and a half, swan, half-pike and back. Laughing the whole time. It was wonderful until….red lights and sirens were heading our way.

At first I thought it was a fire, until I heard the loudspeaker: "We know you are out there. We have your clothes. There are seven police cars from two counties. Come in and give yourself up."

Denise sure knew what she was doing when she swam back earlier, I thought. Penny and I jumped in the water and hid under the dock as the searchlights scanned the small lake. *Come in? Were they crazy?* My dad had been the city attorney. No way, Jose! I would drown before I would show up naked in front of a group of policeman.

I later learned that Denise had gotten her clothes back on in time and was hiding in the bushes while Beetie was dealing with an empty bottle of vodka that rolled out from under the seat when, after trying for a getaway, she had to pull to a stop for the police.

I still don't know where that bottle came from. It wasn't ours, but try to convince a policeman of that when you have two naked girls in the lake, one of which was inebriated. They checked my car registration so they knew who was out there. The Homecoming Queen of Blooming Prairie, who was also the town attorney's daughter and had been a majorette for the high school band. And she'd dragged one other majorette and a cheerleader down with her. I'm sure the police had run-ins with my father—he was always helping young kids in trouble with the law for free. Now it was time for revenge.

"I can't believe we're in this mess!" Penny said. To say she was not happy is an understatement.

"I think it's funny," I said. Penny dunked my head when I started laughing.

"What are we going to do? They have our clothes."

"Let me think." I started laughing again and Penny had to give me a second dunk.

"Okay, Okay," I said, choking, "I know. We can swim to Dr. Floor's cabin and wake up his son John. He can give us a ride home."

"Where's his cabin?"

"Over there." I pointed across the lake.

"I don't know if I can swim that far."

"It's closer than you think."

We started swimming towards the cabin. Penny got tired and I told her to get on her back and I would do the fireman's carry.

"You're naked. No way," she said.

"Naked or drowning? Take your pick."

She did as I said. It was a long way across that lake, but we arrived at Dr. Floor's boathouse in good shape. Those years on the women's university swim team paid off for me.

"Let's see if there are some towels or something in here to cover ourselves," I said as I climbed up on the dock.

The only thing I found was Dr. Floor's fishing vest. I put it on. It barely covered the areas that needed to be covered, but it would have to do. I promised Penny, who didn't have anything, that I would get a hold of John and be back to get her. She had her reservations.

I threw some rocks at John's window. A voice answered and told me to come to the front door. Yes, my plan was working. We would escape! As the door opened, I was in for a big surprise.

"Hello, can I help you?" It was Dr. Floor. "Isn't that my fishing vest you're wearing?"

"Uh…ya… I'm just borrowing it for the moment," I said, crouching a little to make sure everything was covered.

"Is all the commotion out there about you?" he asked.

"Um, I think so. It's my 21st birthday and I thought I would go for a swim. My clothes are on the beach. I think the police have them."

"Aren't you Kathy Thorson? I think your mom is a patient of mine."

"Ah…yes. You aren't going to say anything to her, are you? She has enough on her mind with my dad's recent death."

"No, I won't. We need to get you some warm clothes," he said. We heard a shout from upstairs—his wife asking who was at the door this late at night. He shouted back that it was a friend of John's and that everything was under control. Thank goodness she didn't come down! Dr. Floor went upstairs and came down with a sweatshirt and pants.

"Do you have another set of clothes?," I asked. "My friend is in your boat house and she's probably getting a little cold. Oh, and can John Junior give us a ride home? It's my birthday and that would be a really great present right now."

He hesitated and then said, "I guess so. He needs to come right home after dropping you off."

He went back upstairs to get another sweatshirt and pants. I headed down to the boathouse with the clothes in hand. Penny was not happy when I got there. She thought I'd taken too much time. I explained to her that it's important to be patient and humble when the power isn't in your hands.

John was happy as hell to see two wet-haired girls wearing his clothes in the middle of the night. We jumped in his car and took off down the road toward town. A little ways down, I saw my car on the side of the road.

Beetie was inside. "Look what I have," she said, handing me a ticket.

I looked at it. "Don't worry. I'll get you out of it or at least pay for it. I have a job."

The next day, we went to Chuck Ellis, the city magistrate, with $150 and the ticket. I'd cleaned out my savings account.

I explained to Mr. Ellis that the bottle was my brother's and that we didn't know it was under the seat. Beetie was having a minor heart attack knowing her family would be very upset with points on her driving record for Open Bottle. Mr. Ellis accepted my story and he took the money. He had been a friend of my father's. There were never any points on Beetie's driving record and there was never a record of the Open Bottle fine or any reporting in the local newspaper. That was okay with me and Beetie, too.

Yes, it had been a bit of trouble for my friends, but they forgave me. And I had a great skinny dip in Beaver Lake for my 21st birthday. It was worth it!

Traveling in India

A Flower Child's Trip to India

When I was twenty, my mother, my brother Ty, my younger brother, Ronny, and I were invited to Prashant, a coconut and cashew plantation in Kerala, India. Our host, Shri Krishniji, otherwise known as Baba, was a mystic or holy man. He had taken a vow of silence in his early twenties. Over the years, he'd devised his own two-handed sign language to communicate through an interpreter, and was also able to write fluently in English.

A few years earlier, while I was away at college, Baba happened to be vacationing in Minnesota with a couple who had spent a year with him in India. My brother Ty knew this couple, and heard about the holy man who was visiting them. Ty felt it would be helpful for our dying father to meet Baba. This was during the Vietnam War, and my two older brothers, Steve and Gary, were in the Navy on secret missions. When I returned home from college, I heard about Baba from India and was very curious about him.

When my mother accepted Baba's invitation to travel to Prashant in September 1973, I was able to arrange an independent study abroad program through my university so I could go and still be working toward my degree. I was anxious to spend time with my family—well, at least my mom, Ty and Ronny—since my father had recently passed away. It was an opportunity of a lifetime.

It was also a needed retreat for my mother, after the extended time she had taken care of my father, who'd battled diabetes, throat cancer and bone cancer for the past ten years.

When we arrived in India, my mother, Ty, Ronny and I discovered that we were sharing the plantation with another American couple who were on a spiritual quest.

At first, I didn't know there was a Shrine of Silence that had been built on the property for meditation purposes and was surrounded by beautiful vegetation. I'd seen these plants in greenhouses back home, though certainly not the size I saw here. The jackfruit, papaya, mango, cashew flowers and plantain trees were my favorites.

The Shrine of Silence was in its own secluded area about one block from the house. When you approached, the ten-foot-high, one-foot-thick, hand-carved, rosewood doors, they appeared to be standing guard over the interior. You washed your feet and stepped into a smooth, marble cave that was shaped like a mother's womb; then sat in a yogi position on a high-density, hand-knotted, oriental carpet from Kashmir. The shrine was lit by a stream of light that poured from a hole in the ceiling of the lava rock through a 240-carat yellow topaz gem—quite a dazzling experience. If I went now that I'm older and more mature, I would have enjoyed the daily meditation ritual.

At the time, it was boring, because the rule was, you didn't talk inside the shrine, or even move. You sat and you meditated. Sometimes I was so bored I wanted to bring a few scorpions in just for some excitement.

As I said, I was twenty years old—I didn't know what the word "meditate" meant. I'd never heard it before. There was no meditating in Blooming Prairie, Minnesota.

When I look back at our time in India, the smells are what I remember the most—burning palm leaves, coconuts drying on the roof of the thatched huts, and curry drifting through the open air kitchen. The extreme heat and the pungent, musky smells made the air thick. We were there in the winter, the dry season for this area that is just above the southern tip of India, approximately one mile off the Arabian Sea. It was a jungle. People watched for tigers at night.

Amma (Malayalam dialect for Mama), the mother of the house, was in her sixties. I can remember her in her cotton print sari—appropriate for the daily chores—busy grinding the rice flour for the fresh chapattis that she rolled out on the stone bench. She was plump, with an inquisitive look and long grey hair that she wore in a Malayalam knot.

Amma always had a smile for the guests, but she was stern with the servants. She had one eye on what she was doing and the other eye on the wood fire where a pot of Malayalam potato soup simmered. (I loved that soup.) In addition, Amma had to grind her black pepper, coriander and cinnamon after gathering it from the garden.

Raman, one of the many servants, milked the cow next to the courtyard daily as a woman with a basket of fish on her head patiently waited for Amma to barter with her for the catch of the day. Another servant gathered eggs from the nests of the chickens and ducks that roamed the garden. Other female servants quietly swept a mixture of charcoal, dried cow dung and water drawn from the open well with their handmade brooms, coating the floors of the huts and the raised walkways to deter insects, scorpions and snakes. It worked fairly well. There were no windows or doors in the main house, just a lazy ceiling fan that worked for the couple of hours they had electricity. The dining room held a table and two long wooden benches.

The two-room, thatched hut we slept in was located about a block away. The furnishings consisted of three palm leaf-woven cots that were three feet wide and six feet in length. This was plenty of room for a native, but a little tight for Americans. My brother Ronny took the cot by the door, and Ty took another one. The last one was our cot. Yes, you heard that right, our cot. My mother and I shared a cot and slept head to toe. Believe it or not, I was glad to have had her in the same bed, because every so often, the black and white rats that ran circles on our thatched roof would miss a step and fall through the ceiling in the middle of the night. It would scare the be-geezus out of me, even if the rats were more afraid of me than I was of them.

Other than this rustling sound, it was deafeningly quiet in this quaint place—no planes, cars or electric appliances. It was difficult to get used to at first; however, when I returned home, I couldn't stand how noisy it was in America.

We weren't there in monsoon season, but we still had to walk on the narrow, elevated clay pathways to avoid snakes or scorpions that might be hiding under the dense brush. The doctor's office was a 24-hour ride in an open air taxi, a little too far to make it alive if you had been bitten. The scorpions were large and dark gray in color and the only thing that seemed to bother them were the emaciated yard cats. This was the reason you bathed and did your business in the bathhouse during the day.

The vegetation was lush in this jungle, but every so often you could get a glimpse of the white King Cobra with the smiley face on his hood as he sunned himself high up in the crotch of a hopei tree. He was considered good luck by the locals. I wasn't too sure about that. I figured it was better luck if he wasn't there at all, but what did I know? I was just a kid, an American one at that.

Amma's husband, Appa (Malayalam dialect for Papa), a thin and wiry, old man, was in his seventies. His face was weathered, but he had a very sweet aura.

"Tea and biscuits. Come now while the tea is hot." Appa's squeaky, old voice would announce to the family that it was time for four-o'clock tea. I loved the way the tea was made, in a pot of water that boiled over a fire. It would brew for about three minutes—not too long or it would be bitter. Then a servant would add milk and sugar that was also heated. It was important that the tea be served hot. It was delicious. The biscuits were actually thin shortbread cookies.

When Amma and Appa had guests, everyone gathered in the courtyard at four o'clock.. I loved this ritual. I was greeted by this frail man with the stature of Gandhi and a smile that hung on to that remaining tooth as he grinned from ear to ear. His kind and loving demeanor made you feel that you had known him all of your life.

"Katiana (his nickname for me), let's play a game of chess," he'd say. As he arranged the pieces on the board on the small table in the courtyard, he'd place a black and white piece in each hand to determine who would play first. "Pick a hand."

"No fair, you always win. It doesn't matter whether I get white and get to go first," I'd wine as I plopped down on the stool next to him.

"Now you know what you have to look forward to when you get old. You will win also."

Appa always had some comment or moral lesson to share, but I enjoyed the fact that he cared enough to give me the fatherly attention I craved. "Show me some new moves so I can beat my brothers when I play them."

"Oh, you're such a silly girl. You don't compete with your brothers. They'll take very good care of you. You have to be a lady."

I was a very independent tomboy and I had to be a girly-girl here. It drove me crazy, which, in turn, drove everyone crazy.

Later on in life, I learned very well how to be a girl, but I never had a problem working with tools, driving big trucks or stacking bales of hay. Lucky for me, we didn't live in India, where I would no doubt be reprimanded my whole life for my unladylike behavior.

Table Manners

My table manners were lacking when I was growing up. I mean, so lacking that my boyfriend had to inform me that you don't spread the ketchup on your hamburger with the end of the bottle. I still remember the look on his parent's face as the thick, red sauce dripped down the sides until it reached the label—right where you grabbed the bottle.

The depth of my understanding of table manners was that you better be the first one at the table or there may not be any food left. (Remember, I had four brothers and parents preoccupied with the hard working life.) If I got to the table early in the morning, I not only was able to eat the best cereals, I could surround myself with the boxes and find out what gifts were available with which box top. No wonder that, when I went to India, I was clueless about my own inappropriate manners, much less theirs.

It was a culture shock when it came to what was on the menu in India. No pizza, hamburgers, French fries, macaroni and cheese—or anything else that was palatable to a teenager. The family that hosted our stay in India tried to cater to my food preferences, but they weren't very successful, considering they only cooked their traditional dishes. I had to learn how to eat curries, rice, potato soup and eggs with my right hand. No forks. No meat, except for fish. The spices were so foreign to me—curry, cardamom, cumin, turmeric, saffron and peppers. Hot peppers. The kind that would make your eyes water.

I would see a dish of vegetables and put a portion on my plate, not realizing that it was a spicy chutney that would feel as though it was removing the first layer of my tongue when I ate it. I'd grab my water, choke, grab my mother's water, choke some more, cough, then grab the yogurt and try to curb the burn. If I'd had better table manners, I would have tried to choke more quietly. (I learned not to trust anything that was served to me unless I saw someone else in my family eat it first.)

Another custom that I had to get used to was that my left hand was supposed to stay under the table at all times. Oh, and to never shake hands with my left hand. The left hand had its own purpose in India. There was a bucket of water in the outhouse and I had to use a cup of it to wash my private parts with my left hand after going to the toilet. There was no toilet paper—the Indian people thought it was gross that Americans didn't wash after toileting. I was glad to be right-handed!

But back to eating. I would hang out with Amma and watch the servants gather the necessary raw materials used to prepare the meals. The food was delicious when it wasn't overly spiced. Amma didn't allow me to cook, but she'd let me watch.

One day Amma asked me to teach her English. I agreed. So while she was chopping the vegetables, I named each in English and she would say it in her dialect, Malayalam. (There are over 150 dialects in India, so people had to speak Hindi or English in order to communicate with those from different towns or provinces.) After a few lessons, Amma and I became more comfortable with each other. We started joking around.

"Eye," I said one morning as I pointed to my eyeball.

"Eye?" she asked, confused, no doubt because it sounded the same as the pronoun 'I', which I'd taught her the previous day.

"Eye. I. Same," I said, trying to make her understand. She shook her head and waved her finger in protest.

"Nose," I added, pointing to my own.

"Nose," she said as she tried to wiggle hers and laughed.

"Mouth. Teeth," I said.

"Teet," she repeated. The 'th' sound was foreign to her. I tried to emphasize it by sticking my tongue between my teeth and making a very pronounced 'th' sound. She retaliated by sticking her tongue out. We both laughed.

She then repeated the process in her own language for me to learn.

Then my family came in for breakfast—fresh duck-egg omelets and tea.

"Teet. Teet," Amma proudly said, showing off her new English word.

My brothers laughed but my mother wasn't finding it funny.

"Teeth," I repeated, trying to clear up any misunderstanding.

I didn't do any better when I tried to put my Malayalam lessons to use by speaking to the servants or to Amma. Like the time I approached a mother and her chubby, baby boy that we saw while walking on a trail. I made a faux pas by confusing 'Annakootie' and 'Ankootie'. I thought I was calling her child a beautiful baby boy, only to find out that I was calling him a beautiful baby elephant. The mother was offended and walked away.

One evening, my mother and I went to an important dinner in the Blue Mountains at an estate that was owned by the Maharajah of Mysore. There were many dignitaries at the banquet. My mother was invited because she was starting a business in India, Ruby Cup International, and

American investors were rare at this time. I was along for the ride.

I wasn't sure what food would be overly spicy and I didn't have my brothers there to be my taste testers. Not only that, but my mother was seated far away from me at the other end of the table.

The first course looked like pancakes, but instead of maple syrup, they were served with a mixture of extra spicy vegetables. I managed to find a mango chutney that went nicely with the pancakes. Then dahl and jasmine rice was served, along with a yoghurt. The whole time, the men were talking business and Mother and I listened.

At the end of the meal, a waiter brought me a large bowl of bright-red, sweet strawberries covered in fresh cream. I hadn't seen strawberries in months. I took a bite and swirled the delicious mixture of sweet cream and fruit in my mouth, savoring the experience. Finally, a faint taste of home! I hummed and moaned with every bite. The waiter patiently stood next to me.

I can't believe no one else wants this dessert, I thought, not noticing that all the guests were looking at me longingly.

I kept eating the strawberries, commenting on their ripeness and sweet taste. In fact, I played up the moment to the hilt, pretending to have an orgasmic experience. My mother was seated too far away to put a stop to it.

The Indian men at the table were totally confused. They just stared, bent to the side, and passed gas, which was not an abnormal habit in India. I had to bite my lip so that I didn't giggle.

"Wow, this is so good," I said as I finished the whole bowl. (It was, as I said, a large bowl.) My stomach hurt, but every bite was worth it. The waiter took the bowl away. How odd, I thought again, that no one else seemed to want any.

Later, I learned that I was supposed to taste the strawberry dessert, which was a rare delicacy like a fine wine, and then nod for the waiter to dish up a few strawberries for everyone at the table. All twenty people. I was so embarrassed to find this out. My brothers laughed and my mother—well, as usual, she just shook her head. She knew I didn't mean to be a pig.

So, my manners didn't improve in India. It wasn't until I married my husband, Bill, and we joined a gourmet dinner group that I learned the art of fine dining. Bill was mortified when I asked why there were so many forks and spoons at each place setting for a meal that was presented by the Mayo Clinic.

The Cozy Inn, the nicest restaurant in Blooming Prairie, where I grew up, never placed two forks, two spoons, two knives and a small spoon at the top of your plate. And what was with the itty, bitty fork? So, I took a white glove course offered by the Mayo Clinic Fellow Wives to learn the ins and outs of proper etiquette.

I got it down pat and am still delighted when someone asks which fork to use. I point to the correct one and bail them out with a polite smile. I've come a long way.

The Lady in Blue and White

I loved the weather, the fauna, and the family while we were in India with Baba, but the food and customs were very different from my Minnesota home town. I missed the hamburgers, French fries, macaroni and cheese and pizza—oh, how I missed the pizza. The Indian food was spiced with flavors like curry and cardamom that were not on the menu of a typical USA teenager in the 1970s.

One day, Mom announced that we were going to go on a trip and ride the same elephant that Jackie Kennedy rode on a safari through a park that had tigers, giraffes, lions, elephants and other wild animals.

"We've planned to go for lunch at a restaurant before the safari, and Baba has arranged for the chef to make you some pizza," Mom said, knowing that this would give her a lot of bartering power for future good behavior from her independent and not-so-courteous daughter.

"We're gonna have pizza? You've got to be kidding!" I said, jumping up and down. I had regressed to much younger behavior because I had so little independence here.

"I can't wait. Ty and Ronny will be so jealous. When are we going?"

"Tomorrow," Mom said, laughing as she watched me dance in circles. I headed for our hut, knowing that the next day would be special, but, at the time, I didn't realize how very special it would become.

The sun was rising while we drank our Indian tea and ate duck-egg omelets with Indian bread called naan. My mom and I sat in the back seat of the rented, aged Mercedes with Baba's interpreter, Savathri, , while our host, Baba, sat in the front seat with the chauffeur. We had a long drive ahead of us. I'm not sure where the car came from, since I didn't see any cars at Prashant, the plantation where we were staying. The only wheeled transportation available was an open, old jeep referred to as the 'taxi' that came from the small town of Chevatur. It didn't matter. We were on our way for pizza and a safari and I was elated.

Along the way, we passed screeching monkeys, open carts with sugar cane juice, and cows moseying along the road. People stared as we drove by.

"We need to stop at the next town," Mom announced.

The car stopped at a four-room, thatched hut, surrounded by drainage ditches that carried away the excess water and sewage. There was a strong stench of urine and rotten eggs. The doors of the car opened, and my mother and I were shuffled into the small courtyard. The noise of screaming babies was drowning out our conversation. Baba and the driver went to refuel the car.

"Why are we here? When are we going to get pizza as you promised? I'm hungry," I said, growing more impatient as the piercing baby cries seemed to enter the bottom of my spine, creep up my back and explode at my temples.

"I'm here to give a donation," my mother said, giving me the evil eye that meant I was supposed to behave myself.

We approached the baked-clay porch, which had a large basket and bell sitting next to it, and went inside. Cribs lined the walls and also filled the center of the room. A narrow path between the rows of cribs was just wide enough for the nuns who were working there to get to each baby. One nun fed the baby, the next nun changed the baby, and the final nun burped the baby. I watched them move systematically from crib to crib until all of the babies were seen. There must have been thirty cribs in a twenty- by fifteen-foot room.

"Is this a day care?" I asked Savithri.

"No, an orphanage."

I peeked around the corner and saw about twenty-five toddlers playing with old cups and sticks on a dirt floor in the next room, some disabled. Most of them were girls. Every so often, in between the cries of the babies, I heard a bell jingle outside. I figured these were warning bells on bicycles, which seemed to be the usual transportation for local workers.

Then, with no warning, the curtain to the front waiting room opened and a small, frail woman in a blue and white cotton habit entered. The babies were crying as if they were in a competition to see who was the loudest.

I heard a song, weak and limited in pitch due to the aged voice box singing it. One by one the crying babies stopped. The children in the other room came to the door. This four-foot-something old woman picked up each baby and kissed it on the forehead while singing an undistinguishable lullaby. By the time she reached the last baby, the room was completely quiet. I still get goose bumps every time I think about this experience.

The toddlers who could walk rushed to the door that was barricaded by pieces of wood tied together with palm grass. They reached for this woman as if she was their personal 'mom'. She kissed each one of them.

"Wow! Who is that person?" I whispered to Savathri as she watched Mom interact with the woman.

She held up a finger to silence me.

"I would like to leave some money for the orphanage," I heard my mother say.

The preoccupied old woman pointed to a woven basket in the corner of the room for my humble and generous mother to place the money.

"You want me to leave this many rupees in this communal basket?" Mom asked in disbelief. The amount was over $500, the equivalent of a worker's ten-year salary.

The frail but diligent old woman pointed with more emphasis at the straw basket, clearly wanting to make the most of her time with the children. We started to leave the simple, but clean hut, and again, I asked who the woman was.

"Mother Theresa," my mother responded. "She takes care of the orphans and lepers in the community."

I was humbled and given a new reference point of reality that changed my life. Those babies knew something I didn't. I turned around and went over to Mother Theresa.

"Could you give a twenty-year-old girl some advice for my future?" I asked.

"Be the best you can be, whether you are making a cup of tea or saving the world," she said with a meek smile. I thanked her, aware that this woman was special.

As we were leaving, again I heard the bell. I looked in the direction of the sound. A woman with a sari covering her head was hurriedly placing a newborn baby in the large, spiral-woven basket on the front porch next to the doorway of the orphanage. She rang the bell, which I now realized was the signal that a new child had been placed in the basket for the orphanage to take care of. As the woman looked back for one final glance at the baby, she was wiping tears from her face.

And what about the pizza and safari I was promised? I savored every bite with humbleness and gazed at the wild animals with gratitude.

Impropriety in India

The entire time I was in India, I had trouble adapting to the customs and culture. We were living in the southern tip of the country, in a very small village where women were quiet and proper. If I'd been Indian, I would be married with children at my age, so my behavior seemed odd to this family.

I was a tomboy. There probably isn't a word in the Malayalam language for tomboy. Females weren't even allowed to ride a bike. It was considered improper. It was hot, but I couldn't go swimming. You would never see an Indian girl in a one-piece suit, much less a bikini like the one I wore at home.

The customs were so different that even when I tried to do the right thing, I failed. Like the dancing incident. It was a custom in India for children to perform for guests. When I was asked to entertain for some company, I was happy to. I hiked up my floor-length lungi and proceeded to do the Charleston, leg kicks and all. I had learned the dance for a contest at home. I was good.

There was one problem. I had no idea that, in India, it is improper for women to show their ankles. This is considered risqué. The dropped jaws of the Indian men and the popped-out eyes of the elderly wives are still a vivid memory. Even the servants hid their faces as they giggled.

My mother had no idea she was supposed to be embarrassed. She was clapping in time to my singing with a big smile on her face. That smile was gone shortly after the dance was over when Amma informed my mom that my dance was improper and had embarrassed the guests.

The female servants walked around bare-breasted while they worked and the Indian people were worried about my ankles? Again, different customs. What's the saying? *When in Rome, do as the Romans do.*

No, I was not about to walk around bare-breasted while hiding my ankles. I wore a top *and* covered my ankles.

Then there was the time I talked my brothers into going swimming in the Arabian Sea at sunset. We knew it would have to be a secret. Women didn't swim in India. We walked to town after saying we were going shopping, then had a driver take us to the beach.

It was beautiful. The sun was setting over the ocean and the sand was as white as snow. The beach was vacant and there were no hotels, umbrellas or people. Pristine.

One thing was strange, though. The bushes appeared to be moving even though there was no wind. It turned out that news had hit the town that a young, white girl was swimming there. The local men had broken off branches and were watching me from a short distance, hiding behind the greenery. I guess it was rather dangerous at the time, because the Russians were supporting India and the United States was supporting Pakistan during the India-Pakistan war and I could have caused a political scene.

Well, being a small village, it didn't take any time for Baba and his family to hear about our dip in the ocean. This time, I was told I would have to wear a burka: a long black dress that covers the body completely, leaving only eyes exposed. I panicked. It was over 100 degrees during the day. I would die. This turned out to be an idle threat, but it worked to stifle the tomboy in me for a while.

Until I caused yet another scene when I took Raman's bike. I wanted to go for a ride and asked Raman, who was one of the servants, if I could use his bicycle.

He didn't speak English, so he didn't know what I had asked. However, he nodded his head and I took that for a yes.

It was a beautiful ride through the rice fields and lovely gardens. I found a path that went up a steep hill. The rugged, dirt road was difficult, but I was young and fit. People stared at me as I rode by, but did not wave back when I waved to them.

Well, they had a reason. It was taboo for a woman to ride a bike. Again, it was the ankle thing. The family panicked when they learned that I'd taken Raman's bike and had gone for a ride. Twenty people were out looking for me, afraid for my safety.

Raman also panicked when he realized what he had unknowingly agreed to. He managed to find me first and motioned for me to sit on the seat of the bicycle. Then he inserted himself between me and the handlebars and, standing, pedaled us back to the plantation while I held on to the back of the seat. I knew I would've been in trouble if I hung unto his torso. He was a married man, I was a single woman, and that would have caused a stink.

He went as fast as he could back to the plantation. I'd never ridden on a bicycle going that fast downhill. I can just imagine what the people along the road must have been thinking. Maybe that's why he rode the bike so fast.

When I arrived back at Prashant, Appa took me aside and gave me a speech in his kind, elderly style. He was so sweet that I cried and apologized for taking the bike. He told me that my punishment would be one week with no incoming mail.

"No mail? I'll die if I don't hear from my friends and boyfriend!" I cried.

"You must have some sort of punishment for the worry that you gave the people that went looking for you. You weren't being responsible and it's important that you remember this," he said.

Every day Baba said, through his interpreter, "Another letter came today for you. Too bad you can't read it."

I found after my week was over that I hadn't gotten any mail. This way of disciplining me worked.

At least it worked until I was introduced to a twenty-year-old boy that was the son of a highly regarded man in politics. He was cute and so, being the exact same age, I waltzed over to talk to him. I thought he was shy, but he had a smile that was encouraging. He spoke English well and I was having a great time until his father whisked him away. He had been promised to another girl at the age of fourteen in an arranged marriage. He was finishing his studies and then his arranged marriage would be finalized. (That's when I discovered that, at the time, ninety-nine percent of the marriages in India were arranged.) How was I to know I shouldn't have been flirting with him?

There was no one to flirt with on our walks up to the top of the hills that were green and spotted with volcanic rocks. But this was a treat that I treasured every day.

My two brothers and I, along with my mom and the two other guests, would sit and watch the sun set over the Arabian Sea. I learned to appreciate sunsets. We have beautiful sunsets in Minnesota, but you don't have the opportunity to watch the sun slowly sink into the ocean or to see the ocean take on the brilliant pinks that are reflected off the water. I managed to get in a bit of impropriety on these walks, even so.

One day, Jim, another guest at Prashant, was walking the path with us, boasting yet again how he was a millionaire and should be treated like a prince rather than treated like a regular visitor.

Everyone rolled their eyes and tried to ignore him. This was hard to do, as he was very large, obnoxious and spoiled. He was a trust-fund kid.

My brother's dog, Sheen, had come with us to India and was now sniffing in a bush. Just for fun, I said, "Get it, Sheen."

She lunged at the bush, and a huge black snake slithered out, heading directly for Jim, who panicked.

I wish I'd had a camera! He leaped in the air, all 300 pounds of him, and balanced on his walking stick with his feet above his head. We laughed, hard, which only aggravated him more. He wasn't humble and he was here on a spiritual quest. Really? I think the serpent that slithered under him was trying to tell him something.

Baba owned another dog, Lila, a Saint Bernard who'd been a gift and was very sweet—and a novelty. You didn't see registered, large dogs in the community. In general, dogs weren't highly regarded and they mostly looked like thin dingoes.

One day, I decided to take her on our sunset walk, not realizing she was still a puppy. Everything went well until my family and I reached a stone wall that had a large ditch on the other side. Ty and Ronny helped my mother over, and I started to remove the leash that I had tied around my wrist so I could cross. The next thing I knew, Lila had jumped over the wall and I was flying through the air behind her. I landed on top of her on the other side. It was a good thing I only weighed 104 pounds! She weighed more than that and softened my landing. I wasn't hurt and neither was she. A little surprised maybe, but that was all. It gave us a good laugh.

I haven't forgotten the culture, the scenery, the food or the lessons that I learned in this foreign country and I never will.

Living Married in Rochester

Boundaries on the Waters

Life had been tough and my husband Bill and I were ready to go back to nature for peace and quiet. Bill had met two other couples in his residency at the Mayo Clinic and we decided that a two-week canoe trip to the Boundary Waters was in order. I was busy teaching full time and Bill had an 80-hour work week, so time was short and packing would be up to me. I was fine with that.

The other two couples, who were more experienced in this endeavor, thought it was prudent to take a weekend practice trip down a smaller river before we spent two weeks in the Boundary Waters—that area was a very primitive nature preserve. If we forgot something, we would be out of luck.

Jim and Kay, Mike and Paula, and Bill and I arrived at Apple River in Wisconsin with all of our gear for our practice trip. It was a beautiful but crisp day in late May. This was the relaxing time away needed for all of us hard working girls and a grueling residency for the boys—until Bill noticed the new license tag I'd put on the car.

"What does this mean, *Lead the single life, marry a doctor*"? Bill asked.

"A girlfriend sent it to me. I think it's funny."

As the girls giggled, the men ignored us and packed the canoes and we were off for a fun weekend.

Our Apple River trip was uneventful other than the underwear incident. I guess I didn't pack enough "whitee-titees" for my husband since my mama taught me to "let that thing breathe" at night. We had a great time, and it appeared that we were ready for a two-week Boundary Waters experience.

When we arrived home, I told Bill that I was going to unroll our sleeping bags to make sure they would be dry for the Boundary Waters trip.

"Don't touch my bag. I'll do it. I don't need your help," he answered.

"Was it the underwear or the license plate?" I said. "I'm sorry if it upset you."

"I took care of myself for twenty-one years before I met you and I can take care of myself now," he said.

"Okay, if you insist. But if you change your mind, just ask, I'm more than willing to help." I was glad that I wouldn't have to pack for him. He would make time in his busy schedule to get it done.

Two weeks later, it was time for a wonderful nature experience with Jim and Kay and Mike and Paula. It was early June and the weather was brisk.

It would be quite cool in the Boundary Waters in Minnesota. The plus side to this was that the mosquitos would be fewer in number. The chance that those pesky creatures could pick you up and fly away with you was minimal. I've seen swarms so thick in that part of the country that it looked like a curtain—and all of those mosquitos are ravenous. On the plus side, the area is beautiful and pristine. It's a heavily forested natural park with low human impact. No shopping malls. Well, actually no shops at all. You brought in what you needed and took out your trash. It was a great place for a get-away. Let the fun begin.

"Got your duffle bag and sleeping bag packed?" I asked Bill.

"I have everything I need packed. Don't need your help. I've also packed a hatchet, knife, fire starter and the mini camper stove. Can you take care of the coolers, food and utensils?" Bill asked.

"No problem," I said, impressed with his promptness. A little voice told me to check his bag, but I didn't want him to get upset. He sounded so confident. I decided to let it slide.

We arrived at the store where we were renting the canoes around one o'clock in the afternoon. Pictures of

Paul Bunyan and Babe the Blue Ox hung next to the stuffed moose head with sunglasses and a hat with a hole cut out for one of his ears. The solid pine walls with the tree branch railings, along with the other decorations, let me know that we were in Northern Minnesota.

"Which one of you is navigating?" the old man behind the counter asked.

"I am," Jim answered.

"You know if you get it wrong, you can go over a waterfall," the old man said, looking over the glasses that were hanging on the tip of his nose.

"Well aware of that, sir," Jim said.

"Waterfalls?" Are you sure you know what you're doing?" I asked Jim.

"Yes, done this before. Don't worry."

"Oh yes, the definition of worry is the misuse of imagination," I said, making light of the comment and trying to put myself at ease. I trusted my navigational experience, but I had concerns about Bill's ability.

There was one canoe for each couple. Our camping gear and duffle bags were protected inside black plastic bags that were neatly stacked in the middle of the canoe along with the coolers.

"Are you going to wear that straw hat? It'll get wet and fall apart," I said to Bill.

"Yes, I like my hat and I'll be just fine."

"Okay. Just thought you could buy another hat here before we head out, to be on the safe side."

"Not necessary. I like my hat," he said, taking off for the dock.

We put our three canoes in the water and were on our way. Jim and Kay were the leaders since they had the map. Bill and I decided that he'd be in the back of the canoe and I'd be in the front, but we soon found that wasn't working.

"Bill, what are you doing?" I asked as the canoe careened sideways down the river.

"I think I just saw a new bird!" he said, looking through his binoculars while his paddle lay on the bottom of the canoe.

"Grab your paddle. You need to steer. We'll be heading down the river backwards soon. Didn't you learn how to paddle a canoe in Boy Scouts?"

"Never made it past Cub Scouts," he said, still looking through the binoculars.

"Let's switch positions. I was a star canoe navigator in Girl Scouts. That way you can look all you want through those binoculars. We just need to have someone steering,"

We headed to some quiet waters along the shore and were able to secure the canoe next to a fallen tree.

I proceeded to stand up, tuck my paddle under my seat, and make my way over the bundles of garbage bags.

Bill started to do the same—except he hung on to his paddle.

"Put the paddle down," I said, hanging on to the sides of the canoe, trying to stabilize it.

"I like this paddle."

"The paddles are the same and you need to stabilize yourself on the sides of the canoe." I tightened the strap on my lifejacket before sticking my hand in the water. It was cold.

"I think the glaciers just melted! You don't want to fall in this water. I'll go under and you go over me when we get to the middle," I said, realizing that maybe this switch wasn't a good idea. Also, the other two couples were out of sight by this time.

The canoe was wobbling back and forth when Bill started to lose his balance. His hat flew off. It landed in the water and started drifting away. He lunged for it, knocking me flat on top of the garbage bags as he fell on top of me.

He crawled to the other end of the canoe. "That wasn't so bad except I lost my hat."

"Can't wait to see the footprints on my back when we get to the campsite," I said, brushing myself off.

"Sorry. Are you okay?"

"Yes, a little wet and trampled, but I'll survive." Continuing to paddle, we rounded the bend. The other two couples were waiting under a low hanging branch.

They grabbed some drinks and snacks out of their coolers.

"Hungry?" Mike asked. "I see you switched places in the canoe. We were a little concerned when we saw Bill's hat float by."

"Yeah, it blew off Bill's head. It was a little tricky switching, but we made it," I said as I grabbed the plastic bag filled with Gorp: a mixture of nuts, raisins and M&M's.

Mike tossed a couple of colas our way. I grabbed them and handed one to Bill.

"It's beautiful here and so peaceful. I can't believe that we haven't seen another person, house, farm or anything all day," I said as I lay back in the canoe, giving my back a rest. Bill was munching and drinking while he kept looking through his binoculars.

"Bill, what are you looking for?" Kay asked.

"Snipe," Jim said and we all laughed. Bill didn't flinch and continued to look up and down the river for birds or whatever else might catch his eye. I think he knew there was no bird that was known as Snipe. It was a joke.

"How much longer till we camp?" Paula asked.

"About an hour, so when you see a flat place where we can bank the canoes, let me know," Jim said, looking at the map.

The two other couples arrived at a flat place in the river before us and had pulled their canoes out of the water and removed their gear. Bill and I followed suit and began setting up camp.

I grabbed the tent. Bill followed behind with the sleeping bags and pads. We set the tent up in record time. As I was rolling Bill's sleeping bag out, I smelled mold. It was still damp from the previous canoe trip!

"Bill, your sleeping bag is wet. Didn't you roll it out and dry it after our last trip?" I asked.

"I didn't think it was that wet. We can share yours," he said.

"I have a mummy bag. Only one person fits," I said, realizing it would probably be in the lower forties when the sun disappeared.

"I'll just put on some extra clothes," Bill said. "Speaking of clothes, I'm going to get out of these wet pants and shoes and get into something dry before it gets too cold."

I watched while Bill took everything out of his bag. He emptied every pocket and crevice.

"Oh, crap!" he said. "I didn't bring an extra pair of pants or shoes."

I had to turn away so he didn't see the smile on my face as I saw what looked like about forty pair of underwear, along with forty pairs of socks and twenty-some T-shirts. Not good. He sure wouldn't fit into my pants or shoes.

We walked over to the group. They were sitting around a wonderful fire talking shop and the politics of medicine. Kay and Paula had started supper—it was their turn on the schedule we'd made.

"Does anyone have an extra pair of pants or shoes?" Bill asked nonchalantly.

"What!" Jim and Mike blurted out in unison.

"You didn't bring any extra pants or shoes? Really?" Jim asked.

I didn't say a word. I actually felt badly, but I have to admit, I felt vindicated.

"I have a pair of long shorts. They may look like pedal-pushers on you because of our height difference, but you're welcome to them. What shoe size are you?" Mike asked.

"Size eleven."

"I'm a nine," Jim said.

"I'm nine and a half," Mike said.

"I'll go get the pants. You must be getting cold in those wet pants and shoes. Get some dry socks on. The footing around here is fairly soft and I think you can go shoeless," Mike said.

Mike brought the pants and Bill went back to the tent to change. The rest of us went over to the make-shift kitchen to get ready for supper. Bill returned with his new pedal pusher shorts. I saw him fiddling around the campfire, but I wasn't sure what he was doing. Maybe trying to warm up.

"Come on, Bill. Food's ready," I said. "It looks good and I know you're hungry."

We were sitting on top of the coolers in a circle talking about the next day's trip down the river when, all of sudden, there was a huge flare in the campfire.

"Damn. My pants and shoes!" Bill screamed.

Bill had had used a forked tree limb, braced by another large stick that leaned over the top of the fire, as a "clothesline." His wet pants were draped over the thickest part of the limb and he'd put one shoe on each of the forks. Now, his pants were on fire and the rubber on his tennis shoes was melting.

He ran over and, using another stick, flung the burning pants and shoes out of the campfire. The only thing that drowned out the crackling fire was the sound of laughter coming from Mike and Jim.

It took all of my strength not to laugh with them. I ran over to help Bill and to see what could be rescued. The pants were a total loss. The shoes? Well, the rubber on both the tennis shoes had melted to a point, which made them look as if they'd be appropriate for a genie. They were just missing the tassels.

One look and I burst out laughing. Kay and Paula joined in. The only one who wasn't laughing was Bill.

"I think you'll still be able to wear the shoes," I said, trying to bring some light to the mess.

Bill took his genie shoes to the tent and came back to the campfire. After telling some stories and jokes, everyone decided to go to bed. Tomorrow would be a long day on the river—there were many portages and rapids. I snuck back to the tent to hide the binoculars. Bill was going to have to pay attention on this run.

"Before you get into your sleeping bags, make sure you zip your tent tightly. You may find a skunk in your tent if you don't. Also keep a flashlight handy," Jim yelled.

"Skunk? Are you kidding me? That's all we need," I yelled from inside the tent.

When Bill came in, I said, "Sleep with your shoes on. We may need your special genie powers to make the skunks disappear."

I laughed, but Bill didn't find it very funny. "My sleeping bag is wet. We'll need to get into yours."

"I told you it was a mummy bag. We can try, but I don't think we'll both fit."

I zipped the bag completely open and lay down on it. Bill lay down on top of me.

"Okay. Zip the bag," he said.

"Really? How? You're on top of me and I can't reach the zipper. This isn't going to work. I can't breathe."

I had an idea. "Lay your sleeping bag on the ground, and put some of your underwear on top so the dampness doesn't bother you," I suggested. "Then I can lay on top of you with my sleeping bag on top. I think that'll work."

"Okay." Bill carefully counted out eighteen pair of underwear so he would have twenty-two for the rest of the trip. That would give him two pair a day. He placed each one on top of the sleeping bag as if he was preparing a pizza. I'd been camping many times, but this was the weirdest thing I'd ever seen. "All done," he said.

Before I zipped the tent securely, I took the flashlight and gave one sweeping look outside checking for any critters. Especially skunks.

Bill, dressed in a couple of sweaters, his coat and two pairs of socks. He laid down on his underwear bed. I snuggled on top of him pulling my bag over both of us. We were tired and it didn't take long before we were fast asleep.

Sometime in the middle of the night, I must have rolled over and Bill had awakened. His legs were cold. He slowly unzipped my sleeping bag and he slipped his legs inside. In my twilight sleep, I felt hair rubbing against my leg. I sat up and screamed. "Skunk! Skunk! Skunk!"

Bill tried to cover my mouth, but within a minute, the rest of the crew had surrounded our tent.

"Where is it? "Can't see it," Jim said, flashing the light in all directions. He pointed his flashlight into the tent. "What's with all the underwear?" he asked.

"It's not a skunk. " Bill said. "I tried putting my cold legs in the bottom of her mummy bag."

"You still have enough energy for some hanky-panky? Wow, it must have taken you forever to get that many pairs of underwear off," Mike said, as he and Jim laughed. The girls joined in. I was hoping that they didn't think Bill wore that many pairs of underwear at one time.

"I can't believe you did that. I'm totally embarrassed," Bill said as he rearranged his underwear bed.

"I was dreaming and when I felt the hair on my leg, I guess I went into skunk mode. Sorry."

Morning came quickly. We packed up, cleaned the camp sight and headed for the canoes. Bill was standing in front of our canoe waiting for me to get in. I'll never forget this image.

I should've taken a picture. There was Bill in his pedal pushers, genie shoes, a makeshift T-shirt wrapped around his head with the sleeves positioned so it looked like he had ears, and lo and behold, his binoculars around his neck. I guess I didn't do a good enough job hiding them. Oh well, here we go!

A Fish Out of Water

We were short in making our budget, and it was my fault. My husband wasn't happy because we were on risk insurance due to my lead foot. I felt that I should come up with the extra money to pay the car insurance.

So I took the position of head volleyball coach at the public school where I was a speech therapist. Never mind that I'd never played volleyball—I had a coaching certificate. It was for coaching swimming, which I'd done in college. I was a fish out of water when it came to any other sport.

This was at the beginning of Title Nine, when schools were first required to have a female sport available when there was a male sport offered. Our school wasn't going to get rid of football, so it was my job to start a girls' volleyball team.

It wasn't cool for girls to be in sports in those days. Girls were popular if they were cheerleaders, majorettes, flag girls or in the band. When I made the announcement for the new volleyball team on the school intercom, only three girls showed up. All of them obviously not athletic. I went to the superintendent to let him know there wasn't enough interest. He demanded that I develop a team. They weren't cancelling football, so they had to offer this sport. I told the three girls to each bring a friend and that I was throwing a party for them. It worked. I had the minimum of six girls I needed for a volleyball team. Now what?

I went to a neighboring school that had a volleyball coach. She was a lean six feet tall and her hair was cropped short. She was shocked that I was going to coach a team when I'd never seen or played the sport.

I told her I had a week to learn before our first game. She said it wasn't possible. I told her I agreed, but I didn't have a choice. She gave me exercises the girls should do prior to playing the game. She explained the positions, the spike and, of course, the scoring. I took notes but it didn't mean much to me when I came home. I bought a book, but it mostly contained plays and coaching strategies that weren't appropriate for a beginner. I would have to fake it. *Fake it till you make it*, I thought.

The day came for our first game. One of the six girls came to me and said she couldn't play because it was "that time of the month." I said okay. I still had five girls. I'd played badminton and it didn't matter that much if you were missing one player.

I wanted the girls to look good to the auditorium full of people as they came out of the locker room. My idea was to have them run up and touch the top of the net before proceeding to the bench. The first girl fell, the next just threw her arms up and touched the bottom of the net, and the other three walked straight to the bench. They wanted to save their energy. So much for that idea.

The referee informed me that I needed another player. The rules were that I had to have six. I instructed one of the cheerleaders from our school to suit up. She said she'd never played volleyball. I told her that made two of us. She wore the uniform of the girl who couldn't play. I had to take my belt off and put it on her to keep her shorts from falling down. I was already stressed and the game hadn't started.

I looked at the other team and couldn't help but notice that all the girls were tall, thin and muscular. I looked at my team—they were short, fluffy and fluffier. Not good!

"Okay girls, let's huddle," I said.

"What for?" one of the girls asked.

I hadn't thought that out myself. I didn't have a clue, either.

"For team spirit!" I said. We huddled and I had them jump up and down.

"Okay, girls. Follow me." I went out to the court and asked each girl to stand where I was pointing. I showed them how to stretch out their arms in order to hit the ball. I looked around and the referee had his mouth wide open. I could tell he was wondering what was going on.

He walked toward me. "What are you doing?" he asked.

"Getting my team ready to play."

"Don't they know their positions?"

"Not yet. We're working on that," I said with a smile.

"This is your A squad and you're the head coach?" he asked, even more confused.

"Yep, and don't underestimate us," I said, wishing that was true.

The game started and we lost the serve. That was okay. I wasn't sure I had anyone that could get it over the net anyway.

The ball came over the net and landed just short of one of my players. She didn't move to try to hit it. In fact, no one on my team tried to move to hit the ball. The other team scored twenty-one points in a row.

My girls were still holding their arms out in front of them hoping a ball would land on their arms when the whistle blew and we had to switch sides. The girls came in for a drink of Gatorade and to talk about the next plan, but there was no plan. I just wanted them to hit the ball at least once.

After the break, we had the serve. The first girl hit the ball and it went over the net. The other girls were jumping up and down, so excited that we got the ball over the net. When the ball was returned, they weren't paying attention and we lost the serve.

The other team served the ball and one of my girls accidently hit it in the air. She then went after it and hit again. The whistle blew.

"What's wrong?" I asked.

"A player may not hit the ball twice in succession," the referee responded.

I took note of that rule and was wondering how many more we would break before the night was over. A girl from the other team served the ball again. It hit the net and went over to our side and hit the floor.

"Net ball," I screamed, expecting to get the ball for my team. The referee blew his whistle and came over to me.

"The ball may be played off the net during a volley and a serve. Do you have a rule book?"

"Nope, do you have a spare?" I asked.

He looked at me and I could tell he was getting impatient. I was holding up the game and I thought I'd better keep my mouth shut. A ball was hit again. It landed on the boundary line. My girls pointed to the line, only to find out that it counted against them.

The ball was served again and this time it was short of making it over the net. A girl from the other team caught the ball and the next thing I knew, one of my girls grabbed the ball also and there was a tug of war under the net. The referee blew his whistle. I think my player just wanted to be able to say she touched a volleyball during the game. I wasn't sure.

We served the ball and it was a beautiful play by the other team. A girl set it up and another girl spiked it hard and it landed in front of the second row of my players.

"Is that legal?" one of my players asked.

"Yes, it's called a spike. Keep playing," I said. At least I knew that much.

The season went by pretty much this same way and we never scored a point—until the very last game. We were playing the number one team in the finals. I was dreading it, even though I was used to not scoring by now.

We got the serve to start the game, and the next thing I knew, we scored. The ball seemed to miraculously land on the arms of each of my girls and they managed to get it over the net. They did it again, again and again. I believe the girls actually leaned how to play and had improved in their performance.

We won the game. We beat the number one team. The girls were so excited that they ran over and put me up on their shoulders. The stadium was laughing and applauding. The referee was blowing his whistle because we had another game to win in order to win the match. Of course, the girls lost the next two games. They didn't care and neither did I. They had won one game by the grace of God.

At the end of the year, I had to give certificates to each of the girls at the final awards banquet. I was proud because none of my girls quit. In fact, three more of their friends joined. I had a party at the end of every week after practice and maybe that's why they stayed. We played music on my record player and ate pizza and brownies that I supplied. Food was definitely their motivator. We had great talks and laughs.

When I was at the podium to make my head volleyball speech, I wondered what I could say to a room that was dominated by men. When I started my speech, I was shaking badly and it felt like my mouth was full of cotton balls.

"Hello, I'm so glad to talk to you today as the head volleyball coach. It was a learning curve for everyone. We had a zero to sixteen season."

There were a few snickers, but most of the people in the audience were respectful. I went on.

"It took me awhile to feel up the team…." The participants in the gymnasium started to laugh. I had no idea why they were laughing. I assumed it was because of our record.

I went on. "It took a while, but I could tell who the best ball handlers were."

The audience roared with laughter. I was clueless. My team was laughing so hard they were barely able to sit up straight. I guess my speech about girls handling balls in a room full of men was funny to them.

Then I froze. I forgot what I was going to say. I looked out at the audience and I said, "Whoopee for them. Give them a hand!"

The whole place began to clap and the girls stood up and bowed in all directions. It was a great experience, but I still don't have any idea how to coach volleyball.

Black Grubs

I taught English as a Second Language to employees of IBM that were training in the US for one year. I enjoyed the interaction with the families, but it was also a challenge considering the fact that most of them spoke very little conversational English.

I had my first meeting with Yoshi Sakomoto. He was a young, single man and it was his first experience in America. His dialect was so strong that he really displayed the stereotypical Japanese sound errors. You know, "flied lice" for "fried rice," "Betty nice" for "very nice." etc. This job required a considerable amount of patience. It wasn't one I would recommend for menopausal women or mid-life crisis men. After I completed his evaluation, I set up a schedule for his future lessons. It was after I headed home that Yoshi's story became more interesting.

"Hi, honey, I'm home. That was an exhausting English session," I called as I entered the door.

My husband didn't answer. He was on the phone.

"I think this phone call is for you, but I'm not sure." He handed me the phone with a puzzled look.

"Hello?"

"Yoshi Sakomoto," was the only reply.

"Hi, Yoshi, how can I help you?" I had just left his apartment and thought he understood everything and was fine with his schedule.

"Gabs……Gwabs…….Gawabs." He kept repeating himself with additional letters and accelerating frustration.

"Grubs?" I was familiar with the w for r substitution in the Japanese language. Entomology was not my thing, but I wanted to help. I thought he was saying 'Grubs' but I wasn't totally convinced.

"No Gwubs…GWUBS!" He was obviously disgusted with these tiny maggots. I sensed his fear.

"Yoshi, the grubs won't hurt you, they are little, tiny fly babies. Let me tell you what to do."

My husband was looking at me in total disbelief. I think I was gaining a little more respect for my occupation. He'd see how difficult my job was. I covered the mouth piece of the phone and I whispered to my husband, "How do you kill grubs?"

"Tell him to spray Raid insect killer," he said.

I had a feeling that this explanation might be a little difficult to get across, but I was willing to try. I wanted Yoshi to know that Americans are helpful and patient people. He was terrified to have traveled here to our country because of all the news of guns and murders. This was my chance to let him know he had a support system in America. I loved that *to the rescue* feeling.

"Yoshi….Raid….No….grubs." I was pausing between words to give him enough processing time. I turned away from my husband so I could concentrate.

"No red….black gwubs," Yoshi replied.

I swung around and said to Bill, "They're black grubs. I have never seen or heard of black grubs. What do you think they are?" I was alarmed myself.

"It doesn't matter what type of grub, tell him to spray Raid to kill the bugs."

Oops! I knew Yoshi had difficulty deciphering vowel sounds, and would think I was talking about the color 'red.' It was time for me to spell the words. I also realized that I was pushing my husband's buttons as he buried himself in his newspaper and ignored my conversation completely.

"Yoshi….spray RAID…R…A…I…D…It will kill grubs." To make my point, I took the phone and tapped the table top a couple of times, repeating, "Kill black grubs."

I spied my husband looking over the top of his newspaper. I realized that this must look ridiculous.

"Kaaaahteeee (Kathy)…Nooooo (no) keow (kill) gwubs….gwubs on kitten (kitchen) taboo (table)." Yoshi's frustration was spiraling.

I was very concerned. I didn't remember seeing any insects flying around his apartment. Maybe he was opposed to the chemicals in the pesticide? After all, who wants to eat on a table sprayed with Raid?

"Yoshi, take paper and push grubs away. Push them off the table. Spray Raid." I grabbed a portion of the newspaper that my husband was reading out of his hands and rolled it up in a cone shape. I wasn't sure if I was reducing my own frustration by making a scraping and swishing motion on the counter for Yoshi to hear over the phone or if I needed a visual of what I was asking him to do. *Did I really think this was going to get my point across?* Again, I was busted by my Peeping Tom husband as he looked over his shrunken newspaper.

"Kahtee, no gwubs." Yoshi slowly started spelling, "Grubs… Gee-Ow-O-Bee-Eee" Kahtee, Gwubs on kitten tabo."

G-Ow, which would be L-O-Bee, which would be V-E… "Ohhh….OH! MY GLOVES! I left my black gloves on your kitchen table!" The puzzle was solved. I was so happy.

"Yes, yes!" That's all Yoshi could say. He was worn out.

"I'll pick them up at the next English class. Thank you for calling, Yoshi."

I purposely didn't look at my husband, but out of the corner of my eye, I could see he was rolling his eyes and shaking his head.

"You'd better quit doing that with your eyes. They'll permanently stay like that," I said. I love the silly expressions my mom ingrained in me.

Room 333

It was over eighty degrees when my husband Bill and I left the airport and boarded our shuttle to Montego Bay, Jamaica. It was hot—fifty degrees hotter than our home in Rochester, Minnesota. The shuttle driver offered us a special treat, Jamaican punch, which was served in Dixie cups. I was so thirsty, my cup was never empty for the entire fifty-minute ride to the resort.

Bill was very excited because he was a keynote speaker in reference to his arthritis research, and he'd been working on his talk for weeks. I was along for the ride and to help him stay calm before his big day.

We arrived at our resort hotel and when I stood up, I was woozy. I had difficulty focusing and I couldn't figure out what was wrong with me. A lady next to me saw me almost fall and helped stabilize me.

"Excuse me," I said, "I don't know what is wrong with me. I guess maybe it's altitude sickness or something."

"We're on an island. It was all that spiked punch you guzzled down," she said.

"That punch was spiked?"

"Yes. Didn't you hear the driver announce that?"

"No, we were the last ones on the bus," I said, trying to figure out how I was going to function in this condition and help Bill get all our stuff to the room.

I held on to the backs of the seats until I carefully stepped down from the bus. I was getting worse every minute. Bill was busy gathering our bags when I yelled to him that I was getting a bellhop to help. I walked as straight as I could by focusing on the bright, green frogs that were painted on the doors of the facility. I needed water. I managed to get to the front desk.

"Could you give me the keys to Bill's room?" I asked the woman at the front desk. She took her time processing my question—or maybe trying to decipher my slightly slurred speech.

"Last name, please," she said, as she gave me a foreboding look.

"I love your accent," I said, trying to mimic her. "Last name, please."

She stared at me in silence. I could tell that this was a woman you didn't want to mess with.

"It's Gruhn. Sounds like goon with an "r" after the "G," I giggled.

She didn't smile and told me the room wasn't ready and we were in room 233.

"Thanks. I need a bellhop for the luggage, please."

"I'm already here with the luggage," Bill piped up, walking up to me as I stepped away from the desk. "What room are we in?"

I looked at Bill and his face kept moving. I had a difficult time understanding him.

"The room number?" he repeated.

"Oh, room. We're in 333."

A bellhop, overhearing our room number, blew a whistle and yelled "333-333-333." We were instantly surrounded by bellhops. They each grabbed a bag.

"I'm going to walk around and check things out around here," I said, not wanting him to know the condition I was in. It wouldn't go over very well. Bill was definitely not drunk.

I took a walk around the perimeter of the resort, enjoying the beautiful hibiscus and bougainvillea. The rich pinks and purples blended together and stood out against the bright white sand. I sat down in a conveniently placed lounge chair and soaked up the sun. I was in heaven.

After a while, I decided it was time to check on Bill and to make sure all the suitcases arrived in our room. I started to head for the elevator when I realized that I didn't remember the room number and I didn't have a key. I must have given the key to Bill, I thought. I went back to the front desk to request a key.

"Hi, we meet again," I said, sounding a little more sober this time. "I can't remember my room number and I don't believe I have a key."

"I'm not surprised," she said without looking at me. "You're in room 233 and here are two keys. Do you need help with the luggage?"

"No, the bellhops took care of that," I answered.

I went to the elevator and found our room on the second floor. When I entered, there was no luggage or sign of Bill. I decided to take a nap, figuring Bill had decided to take a walk and that the luggage was on a cart somewhere. This place appeared to be safe and secure and I wasn't worried.

I slept a couple of hours and when I tried to get up, my head was pounding. Clearly, I was not handling the Jamaican punch very well. I thought I was going to get sick, but I managed to find some carbonated drinks in the mini fridge. I drank one and it helped my throbbing head. I laid down again until I felt better. By now, hours had gone by, and I was beginning to get worried because Bill wouldn't have left me alone for this length of time. Not that he was needy, but he liked my company. *And shouldn't we get our things settled in our room?* I decided to go looking for him.

I walked the whole perimeter, breezed through the shops, checked out the restaurants, looked in the pool and scanned the lobby—no Bill in sight. I went up to the front desk again to speak to the same woman I'd talked to twice already.

"I'm getting concerned. My husband is missing. He wouldn't have been kidnapped or anything. Right?"

She looked up from her desk. I could tell she was getting fed up and thought I was a pest. "The place is very safe and gated. Your husband has not been kidnapped," she said. "I think he maybe needed a break."

There was an awkward silence. I knew this woman was done with me. There was no help here. I started to walk back to the room when I saw the bellman with the whistle who had ushered Bill away. I walked up to him and tried to describe my husband and ask if he knew where he was. He didn't really understand what I was asking. That's when I remembered telling him we were in room 333. Bill was in the room above ours.

"I just remembered the room number I gave you, 333," I said.

The whistle blew and the bellhop shouted, "333-333-333."

Again, I was surrounded by bellhops who, this time, ushered me down a hallway. I thought this service was a little overdone, but maybe this was how the resort treated all their keynote speakers. I followed. We came to a wall and the bellman touched a button on a remote. The wall moved to reveal a fancy elevator. Now I was worried, but before I could escape, the bellboys, with me in the center, entered. *This must be a special elevator for staff only*, I thought.

I was escorted out of the elevator and chaperoned through a hand-carved cherry door that was nine feet high. As we entered, the view was overwhelming. The room took up the whole third floor of the building, and windows lined all four walls. Ice sculptures of fish and mermaids were scattered among the Chinese Ming vases that held bouquets that were six feet around and six feet tall. The elegant furniture was inlaid with marble and ivory. As I walked around the corner, the thirty-foot table of gourmet food was elegantly decorated with shells, orchids and candles that were four feet tall. The chocolate fountain surrounded by fruit and small cakes was flowing alongside the champagne fountain. The bellman bowed and left.

Bill came around the corner. I was so glad to see him! But then I panicked.

"We have to get out of here. This isn't our room. We're in 233," I said.

"Here, have some champagne and get in the Jacuzzi with me. I've been in and out of there all afternoon. They sure know how to treat a keynote speaker," he said, slurring his words.

I sobered up fast. One of us had to have a brain. "How much of that stuff have you been drinking? Never mind. Get dressed and grab our bags. Like I said, this isn't our room."

Just when Bill was going to start arguing with me, the door flew open and we were surrounded by men holding machine guns.

"Who are you? How did you get the code?" a guy whose face was covered with a mask asked.

"Hi, I'm Dr. Gruhn and I want to thank...."

Before Bill could get another word in, the men surrounded us and started ushering us out of the room.

"Let my husband get dressed. He's covered in just a towel and not very well. He can't go through the lobby like that. He's a keynote speaker tomorrow and people will recognize him."

"This is the presidential suite and we're expecting the president and his guests any minute. He would be very upset if we broke protocol. You have to leave, NOW," he said in a heavy Jamaican accent. "We will bring your bags to your room."

He grabbed the glass of champagne out of Bill's hand and gave him the "look."

"I think you've made a mistake. I'm the keynote speaker...." Bill kept repeating as he wobbled to the elevator, escorted by the man in the mask. The crew followed, with me in tow, guiding us out the door and to the elevator.

As we walked down the corridor to the lobby, I saw that Bill's family jewels weren't completely covered, so I shimmied up behind him to cover his bare private parts. I'm sure it looked a little awkward as I was spooning him through the lobby. Doctors were coming up to us and shaking Bill's hand.

"Can't wait to hear your lecture tomorrow."

"Great topic!" another doctor said as he reached for Bill's hand.

I was so nervous that Bill would forget to hang onto the towel. It would have been a memorable moment if he was shaking hands stark naked among his comrades.

We got to the room and Bill was very disappointed to see nothing but a queen size bed with a TV and a small bathroom. He walked over to the bed, landed on the bedspread and fell asleep.

Bill always thought that I mixed up the rooms on purpose, no matter how many times I explained to him that it was divine intervention so he could experience how people from the upper crust live, even if only a few hours. Clearly, all that Jamaican punch was part of the plan.

Moving to Charleston

Wake Up, Child

There isn't anything more terrifying than when your child is in serious trouble. Been there, done that, got that T-shirt. I had that experience a few times with my oldest daughter, Alice. I was visiting my mother in Blooming Prairie, Minnesota, in January. Not a time I would recommend going. If I remember right, it was below zero with two feet of snow on the ground.

I'd just enjoyed a cup of tea in the early morning and my mother was getting ready for work as I was waiting for my ten-month-old baby girl to wake up. I heard a loud bang. I ran up the stairs and found Alice face down on the hardwood floor not moving. I picked her up and her eyes were fluttering and she appeared to not be breathing. I started CPR and realized she was not coming around. I took off out the door of the house, barefoot, with no coat, to the nursing home across the street. My family was calling an ambulance to meet me there. I was hoping the nursing home had resuscitation equipment.

My brother Tyron followed behind me and was with me at the nursing home. Many of the residents were thrilled to see a baby, until they really looked at her. After a closer look, one resident asked if Alice was dead. I lost it just as the ambulance arrived. We were in the back of the vehicle as my brother told them to rush. I'm sure they were going well over a hundred to get to the Austin Hospital. A neurologist from the Mayo Clinic had been called to meet us at the hospital. The doctor knew my husband, Dr. Bill Gruhn. They had just finished their residencies at the Mayo Clinic before my husband took a position in Charleston, South Carolina. I watched as my baby lay listless on the gurney. Alice opened her eyes as we arrived at the emergency room entrance.

"She's not moving!" I yelled as they whisked her out of the ambulance.

"Please fill out the forms and we need your insurance card," the assistant at the front desk asked.

"My baby is injured and I need to be with her."

"She's with the doctor right now. You'll be with her in a few minutes."

"I don't have my insurance cards with me. I didn't bring my purse. I'll call my mother to get the information. Can I see my baby, please?" I pleaded.

A medical assistant took me around the corner and I heard the nurse say, "They said she wasn't breathing. She wasn't moving. Looks like a normal baby to me. I think the mother is just hysterical. You know how first time mothers can be."

There was Alice playing with the doctor's stethoscope and babbling away. She had a small red mark on her forehead, but other than that, she seemed perfectly normal.

"She wasn't breathing or moving. Honest," I said as I stood there in a robe with no shoes or coat.

The doctor looked at me and said, "Your feet must be a little cold. Where's your boots?"

"I ran across the yard barefoot. I didn't have time to put on boots. Is she okay?"

"Look at her. She's fine. I went ahead and set up an X-ray to be on the safe side, but her reflexes and vitals are within normal limits."

"Thank you. I'll wait in the waiting room," I said as they handed me some hospital socks.

News travels fast in the medical community and my husband in Charleston had heard about everything before I had time to call him and explain.

"Hi, Bill, you wouldn't believe what happened to me today with Alice."

"I've already heard. The neurologist called me. Are you okay? He said you overreacted to Alice falling down."

"What? Overreacted? She wasn't breathing! I wouldn't call that overreacting," I said.

"Well, everything is okay now and just relax. I know it's our first baby and these things can be expected."

"Don't placate me. I'm not some hysterical, neophyte mommy. I worked with babies with special needs. I know when a child is in trouble."

"Okay. Okay. I'm just trying to make you feel better. I love you both and I'm glad Alice is okay."

I stomped around until I realized that I needed to be thankful that Alice was okay. A week later my former nanny, Helen, babysat Alice at her house while I went shopping. When I went to pick up Alice, Helen informed me that Alice had fallen on the steps and had appeared to stop breathing. She was rushing to take Alice to the hospital when Alice suddenly came to and seemed just fine. She didn't need to see a doctor. Helen and her daughter, Genevieve, grew a few grey hairs like I had. We talked about it and had no idea why she went into this minimal breathing state of unconsciousness.

I was taking a bath with Alice in the old ceramic tub in our rental house on Tradd Street. We had finished bathing and I got out of the tub. I was holding Alice's arm on the edge of the tub as I turned to get a towel. She jumped and pulled herself over the tub and landed on the ceramic tile head first. Here we go again. Alice went limp and appeared to not be breathing.

I wrapped my wet, naked body in a silk robe and with Alice wrapped in a towel, I ran to Roper Hospital a couple of blocks away. We had only one car at the time and with the traffic in downtown Charleston, I knew it would be faster to arrive at the emergency room on foot. I told the medical assistant at the front desk to call my husband and I gave them his number and my insurance information. The next thing I knew, a large, African American nurse called me into the room. The doctor had examined Alice and she was fine. Just like before. The nurse looked at me in my silk robe, soaking wet.

"Lordy, child, that robe isn't hiding much. Tell me what happened."

I explained what had happened and that it had happened two other times. I told her how terrifying it was and that I wasn't imagining anything. It was real.

"Of course it's real, honey child. Why, I seen this before. You see, the nervous system shuts down and it's like it has to wake up to get going again. So, this is what I want you to do the next time she does this. You grab the bottom of her foot like this. And you slap it and say, 'Wake up, chillin'. Wake up, chil'.' You understand me?"

"Yes, I do. I hope it never happens, but if so, I know what to do. Thanks."

I walked home completely embarrassed, but again, thankful that Alice was okay. I wasn't too sure about that nurse's explanation or remedy, but it was more information than anyone else had given me. Bill came home late that night from work after Alice was asleep. He told me as I greeted him at the door that he'd had a hard day. Clearly, he wasn't the only one.

"I heard you were at the hospital today," he said. "Are you having a problem? Are you needing attention? I'm concerned that you keep showing up at the emergency room and Alice is fine. Do you need a counselor or something?" he asked.

I was trying to control my anger and frustration. He hadn't experienced what I'd experienced and so I was trying to give him the benefit of the doubt.

"Like I said, she wasn't breathing and I'm going to do whatever it takes to make sure she's okay."

"Could you wear something more than a thin, silk, wet robe if you go to the emergency room? It's the talk around the hospital," he said.

"Oh, don't worry. I won't wear the robe. I'll be stark raving naked next time!" I said.

"I like the idea of stark naked right now,' he said.

We both looked at each other and started to laugh.

A few weeks passed and life was back to normal. The gossip had subsided about Dr. Gruhn's crazy wife and I was getting ready for Alice's first birthday. Bill was playing with Alice upstairs on the bed. He was holding her in the air above his head when all of a sudden she kicked and flew out of his hands. I heard a bang. I ran up the stairs.

Bill was starting CPR and said, "Call an ambulance. She isn't breathing."

I ran up to Alice, grabbed the bottom of her foot, and in the same dialect as that African American nurse, I said, "Wake up, child. Wake up, child," as I slapped the bottom of her foot.

She came to and started babbling and smiling. I turned to Bill, who was completely white in the face.

"Are you okay?" I asked. "I'm glad you didn't run to the emergency room in your robe. You wanted me to call for an ambulance. Are you looking for attention? Do you need a counselor?" Bill didn't say a word. Alice never did it again and I'm forever thankful to that nurse at Roper Hospital.

The Fish House

My husband, Dr. Bill Gruhn, was on the board of a prominent medical clinic when he was invited to interview a physician from California who wanted to join the group. Bill was given the clinic's credit card with instructions on when and where the meeting would be held. He was to invite another physician and a spouse to provide more opportunity for questions and discussions. Bill invited his best friend, Tom, who was an oncologist, along with Tom's new girlfriend, Karen, a nurse. I was invited, too.

The reservation for the meeting was at the Fish House, an exclusive restaurant that served gourmet dishes and expensive wines. It was the type of place my husband and I went if someone else picked up the tab. Pricey and impressive, it had impeccable service and private, intimate tables.

My husband arrived at the restaurant with the candidate, Jeff, a resident who had just finished his rotation in pulmonology. He had an outstanding résumé and had toured the clinic's facility. I'd arrived early at the restaurant and managed to reserve a private table that had a booth with three chairs on the opposite side. It would fit five comfortably. Tom and Karen came shortly thereafter.

"I'm starved. Haven't had anything to eat all day," Tom said.

"That makes two of us," Karen said.

"Three of us," Bill chimed in.

The maître d' chauffeured us to our table explaining that our four waiters would provide the best service. The first waitress brought the menus and told us about the specials for the night. Everything on the menu was a la carte. The drink waiter served water with lemon and orange slices to each of us. The wine waiter came shortly after and offered suggestions as to the different selections and the specialty drinks of the house.

"I'll have a glass of Chardonnay," Karen said.

"Would anyone else like Chardonnay?" Bill asked.

"Sure, I would," Tom added.

"Count me in since we aren't paying for it," I said.

"I'll just have Perrier water with a slice of lime, thank you," Jeff said.

"We might as well order a bottle. What is the best you have that you would recommend?" Bill asked the waiter.

"Here is the wine selection. I'll be back shortly."

Bill looked at the menu and suggested the Beringer Napa Valley selection. Everyone agreed. The wine waiter returned and he took our order.

"Have you decided what you would like for starters?" the waitress asked.

"Escargot and light on the garlic," Karen said.

"I want the bruschetta." I added.

"I'll have the beet thing," Tom said.

"Tom, it's not a thing," Karen teased. We laughed.

"I'll start with the artichoke and spinach dip," Bill said.

"I'll have the asparagus with the roasted pine nuts," Jeff said.

The wine waiter brought the wine, Bill tested it and the waiter poured a glass for everyone, but Jeff. Soon our appetizers arrived and everyone was busy eating.

"Wow, they didn't give you much. For that price, I should've had a doggie bag," Tom said.

"Tom, this isn't the Golden Corral. Mind your manners," Karen giggled.

The conversation moved to discussions about the call schedule, the management and the seniority in the clinic. The wine waiter didn't want to interfere, so he was only able to reach the glasses in front of Karen, Tom and Bill. He kept their glasses full, but as I was sitting next to Jeff in the booth, the wine waiter wasn't able to fill my wine without interrupting the discussion. When the bottle of

Chardonnay was empty, Bill would nod for another bottle to be brought out.

"Can I get your salad or soup order, please?" the waitress asked.

"I'll have the Caesar. They make it at the table, right?" Karen asked.

"It's our specialty," the waitress said.

"Make that two," I said.

"The same," Tom said.

"Me, too," Bill said.

"I'll have the Caesar, also," Jeff added.

The discussion was primarily between Jeff, Tom and Bill. Karen and I were mostly listening and enjoying our own secrets. The wine waiter kept an eye on everyone's glasses and he made sure they were never less than half full, except for mine.

The salad chef arrived with all the ingredients for a homemade Caesar salad. We watched as he whisked the egg yolks and blended in the other ingredients. He added the garlic and Parmesan to the dressing. He carefully placed the romaine lettuce on the individual plates and we were each served. It was outstanding. Everyone cleaned their plate and the discussion continued. I looked at Tom and he looked a little pale. He became quiet and I was wondering if he was okay.

"I'm going to excuse myself. I'll be right back. Order me the filet mignon. Medium rare," Tom said to Karen.

I was the only one who could see him walk down the hall. He wasn't able to walk straight. He appeared to be drunk. *Maybe he's tired.*

"Can I get your main course?" the waitress asked.

"I'll have the garlic spaghetti with….. I mean linguini with shrimp." Karen giggled as she dropped her napkin and silverware. "Oops. It's okay. I'll just wipe them off with my napkin."

"No, Ma'am, we'll replace it." The waitress grabbed the silverware out of Karen's hand. I looked at her, wondering if she was okay.

"I'll take the special. The autumn squash ravi…." I started to say, but before I could finish my order, Karen interrupted.

"Oh, get Tom a steak. Rare did he say? Oh, sorry, I just didn't want to forget." Karen giggled again.

"The autumn squash ravioli," I said, hoping not to be interrupted this time. "The other gentleman at our table wanted the filet mignon special, medium rare, please."

"Oh, shit, I almost messed up his order. Oh, sorry, that wasn't nice to say. I apologize," Karen said. I could tell she was halfway to never-never land. I was concerned.

"Where's Tom?" Bill asked. "I'd better go get him so he can order."

I grabbed his arm and pulled him back into his chair and said, "I ordered for him. We need your order now."

"I'll have the Rock Cornish game hen," Bill answered as he got up and headed down the hall.

I watched his gait and he was wobbly. It didn't seem like he'd had that much to drink. Maybe he was tired, too.

"I'll have the coconut shrimp, please," Jeff said.

We continued the discussion as I looked down the hall wondering where Tom and Bill had gone. Karen was holding her head in her hands and closing her eyes. All of a sudden she looked up.

"Where the hell are Tom and Bill?" Karen said, much louder than she normally talked. "Damn, their food is going to be here any minute. I'm going to get them."

I watched her walk down the hallway and she was definitely drunk. This wasn't good. It was just Jeff and me at the table. I acted like nothing was happening.

"I bet Tom and Bill got a call. Maybe their pager went off," I said, looking for any excuse possible.

"They're on call?" Jeff asked.

"Oh, no, they've been drinking wine. It would probably be the administrator wanting to know how we were doing," I said.

"The administrator calls the doctors on their pager?"

"Oh, no. That couldn't be." I was sounding worse and worse with each excuse. It was important for me to keep Jeff in the dark about what was going on. The clinic needed him to join our group after his medical training. I was saved when the waitress brought our main course.

She paused and I could tell she didn't know what to do about the other orders. Maybe she knew something that I didn't know. "Go ahead and put their food down," I told her. "The other three will be right back."

"Bon appétit," I said to Jeff. We started eating and I decided to take over the interview.

"What do you like to do in your free time?" I asked. "Let me tell you what there is to do for fun in the area. I have fun down pat."

"I like to surf. Fish. Boat."

"You're at the right place. Wonderful for that," I said.

"How about you?" he asked.

"I love to ride to the hunt."

"What is that?"

"The huntsman of the hunt lays down the scent of a fox and then you cast the hounds, watch them work as you follow them on horseback," I said.

"They do that here? I thought that was only done in England."

"Oh, yes. It's called drag hunting. We don't actually go after a real fox. We follow bottled scent so you can see how the hounds work. No guns. I'll give you a quick idea how it works," I said. I proceeded to slap my hands on my knees mimicking the sound of hoof beats. First at the walk, then the trot and finally the gallop.

"When we hear the huntsman blow his horn," I said, imitating the sound, "the hounds give tongue and try to find the scent." I belted out a few hound cries. I then started slapping my knees at a gallop with every so often not making a sound as I said, "That's the horse going over the jump."

We both laughed and he felt he had experienced a fox hunt. Soon, the maître d' came over and tapped me on the shoulder. I quickly straightened up assuming I was making too much of a racket. He leaned over and whispered in my ear.

"Excuse me, could you come with me, please?" he asked very politely.

"Sure," I said. "Excuse me, Jeff, I'll be right back."

The maître d' took me down the hall and out of sight of Jeff and the other customers.

"We have a problem," he said. "The two men that were with you are in the men's room and I do believe one is sick and the other is singing to him. The woman that is with you also seems impaired. I tried to stop her, but she's also in the men's bathroom."

"Fine. Keep them in there. This guy that I'm with has to finish his meal."

"But…but…Ma'am."

I didn't let him finish. I headed back to the table.

"Is everything okay?" Jeff asked.

"Just fine. Let's eat and they'll be with us soon."

We talked about his life in California and what changes he would expect leaving his medical training. I told him about my life in Minnesota. He didn't know what to say when I told him my mom was dating a guru who had taken a vow of silence. The maître d' came back and tapped me on the shoulder again.

"I'll be right back," I said to Jeff.

I got up from the table and headed back down the hall behind the maître d' until he stopped, once again out of sight of the other customers.

"We have a problem," he said. "The woman that was with you is laying across the front entrance and she's blocking it. We…."

Before he could say another word, I was at the front door of the restaurant. There was Karen sprawled out perpendicular to the sidewalk in front of the glass, front door. She was moaning and groaning. I managed to push the door open just enough, hoping not to hurt her, to be able to get outside.

"Don't move me. Don't touch me. I'm going to be sick," Karen said as she held her stomach and rolled from side to side.

I looked around for help and I knew I couldn't lift her by myself. I grabbed her by her ankles and dragged her under the azalea bushes that were on the side of the restaurant and hid her. She moaned and groaned the whole way.

"I'll be back," I said, but I'm not sure she understood me.

I headed for the men's bathroom.

"You can't go in there," the maître d' said. I ignored him and continued on.

Tom was hugging the commode and Bill was talking gibberish and every so often breaking into song. They were both beyond help. I grabbed Bill's billfold and removed the credit card.

"Keep them in there. I'll get the bill paid and we will be out of your hair, I promise," I said to the maître d' as I headed for the dining room.

"Where's the girl?" he asked.

"She's fine and out of the way," I said. I hoped Karen would stay put until I paid the bill.

I went back to the table and decided to level with Jeff.

"How was dinner?" I asked.

"It was delicious and the conversation was just as good," Jeff said.

"Good," I said. "Well. We have a problem. We have four cars and only two drivers. You and me. I'll have you follow me with Tom's car and then we will drop Karen and Tom off at her apartment. I know where she lives. I'll take you back to the hotel in my car and Bill will come home with me. Deal?"

"Sure. Are they okay?"

"They're fine. Just three sheets to the wind. The wine steward never let their glasses go empty and it got the best of them on empty stomachs," I said.

I paid the bill. Left a very generous tip and had the waitress box up the leftovers.

"I'm going to need your help," I said to Jeff. He followed me to the bathroom as I motioned for the maître d' to join us.

Between Jeff, the maître d' and myself, we managed to get Bill and Tom out of the bathroom and to the cars in the parking lot. We looked like the crew from *The Wizard of Oz*. We literally tossed Bill in my back seat and Tom in Karen's back seat. I'd found her car keys in her purse. I knew what her car looked like, but I didn't have a clue where Tom's car was. They had driven separately.

"Where is Karen?" Jeff asked.

"Follow me. I still need your help."

He walked to the front door of the restaurant.

"No, over here," I hissed, waving my arm toward the azalea bushes.

I grabbed Karen under her arms and pulled her out from the bushes just as a couple, dressed to the nines, were leaving the restaurant. They stopped and stared.

"She's a botanist. Can't keep her out of the flowers," I said, just as Jeff was helping me get her upright. The couple didn't buy my story, but I didn't care. We placed her in the back seat of her car on top of Tom.

"I'll drive slowly and follow me. Karen's apartment is only a few blocks from here." I said, as I handed Jeff the car keys.

Jeff followed me to Karen's and we managed to get her and Tom into the apartment. Luckily, I figured out which key would fit the door. I could still hear Bill singing from the back seat of my car in the parking lot.

I drove Jeff to his hotel and I apologized profusely. He laughed and said he had a good time and that he was fine with it.

Bill went to work and he called me. "I talked to Tom and we're going to tell the administrator what happened."

"Don't do that. I would wait until they come to you. You don't know what Jeff told them," I said.

It turned out that Bill and Tom continued to feel guilty so they went to the head administrator and confessed. They were removed from the board with a letter written to the staff. I told Bill to keep his mouth shut, but he didn't listen.

Jeff ended up taking the position (I knew that would happen) and Karen and Tom got married. I'm not sure if sharing Karen's apartment that night had anything to do with their engagement, but I'd like to think so.

Swamp Thing

"I'll take you on the trip of your life!" I said as we passed the live oak trees draped in Spanish moss. Penny had flown in from Minnesota and was visiting me in Charleston, South Carolina, for a long weekend. I'd managed to have Mrs. Hester take care of the children and my husband was away at a medical meeting. The two of us were ready for some sightseeing and Southern charm.

"I know all the ins and outs of this place. Living here for two years, I'm almost a local," I said to Penny as we headed for Middleton Place Plantation. We toured the beautiful grounds and the stables and Penny was feeling like she should be wearing a hoop skirt and drinking sweet, iced tea. "Hurry, I want you to see Magnolia Gardens just down the road," I said as I pulled Penny out of the gift shop.

We drove up to the Magnolia Gardens gate but were told the place was closed due to a special reservation. I turned to Penny and said, "Spoleto Festival is going on and they're probably putting on a show. We'll go the back way like we're going to the garden shop and they will never know the difference." I swung the car around the corner and drove on the sandy, phosphate drive, avoiding the ruts and swampy edges. As I was driving, I noticed people dressed in army fatigues with branches attached to their helmets and grass strapped to their backs. I figured they must be putting on an army or marine show since Charleston had a military base close by.

We got out of the car and walked around the back of the gardens. Penny was mesmerized by the blooming azaleas and rhododendrons. We peeked through the heavily wooded area to see the miniature horses and cows grazing in the distant field. As we crossed the white bridge over the picturesque pond, Penny pointed to a boy sitting in a boat. We approached the boy and noticed he was bleeding from his head. Instantly I went into the *old lifeguard* mode and ran toward him screaming, "I'm coming! I'll help you! Don't panic!"

As I reached the edge of the pond, the boy looked surprised, and all of a sudden, the bushes around the pond moved at the same time, though there was no wind. I heard a motorized vehicle behind me and turned to see a man on a golf cart shaking his fist in the air. The water began to swell in the pond and a monster sporting green dreadlocks and a funny-looking rubberized plant suit stood up.

"What in hell is going on?" the monster asked. Penny and I were dumbfounded and frozen with fear. The golf cart screeched to a halt next to us and a French man began yelling at the top of his lungs. I had no idea what he was saying.

"What are you doing here? How did you get on this set?" someone holding a large camera asked.

"What are you talking about?" I squeaked out.

"We're in the middle of filming *Swamp Thing* and we want to know who gave you permission to be here," piped up an official-looking woman.

I was quick on my feet and fast with my response. "I'm a friend of Charles Dual and he's the owner of this plantation. I come here frequently and he would be very upset with you if he saw you speaking to me this way." Of course I held my crossed fingers behind my back where they couldn't see them since I was stretching the truth slightly. I knew Charles, but he didn't actually own Magnolia Plantation. He owned Middleton Place Plantation. Close enough.

The woman and the camera man talked to each other and then to the French director.

"I'm so sorry I spoke to you rudely," the French director said in a very thick accent.

"Oh, that is okay," I said as if I were a princess at a ball.

"Please join us while we film the movie," the French director politely said as he waved his hand to the vehicle with the small trailer. "Bring out the champagne and hors d'oeuvres for these lovely ladies."

We sat back drinking champagne and eating caviar while we watched the so-called moving bushes—which turned out to be the people in the army fatigues that I'd seen earlier—give the actors cues to the missed lines. We heard the director yell, "Take one, cut, shoot it again, lighter, wrong angle." We heard the swishing of the water as they tried to keep Swamp Thing from overheating in his rubberized suit in the Charleston, mosquito-infested, summer heat. We were fully entertained by this unusual crowd and their antics.

It was many years later that I woke up on the couch in the middle of the night to find *Swamp Thing*, a B-rated movie, playing on the TV. It reminded me how fun spontaneous adventures can be.

Raisin' Cain

"Do you want a banana with your lunch?" I frantically asked my three-year-old daughter, Alice, as I was trying to get both of us out of the house. She needed to be dropped off at Montessori school and I needed to clean the house before my husband came home from his trip.

"Noooo, I had a banana yesterday!" she yelled as she lay on the floor, kicking her feet and flinging her head back.

"How about raisins to go with your ham sandwich and yogurt?" I asked.

The whining stopped and she slowly accepted the lunch and out the door we went.

My husband had been gone for four days to a meeting and I'd taken a wonderful R&R from housework and my job. I was pregnant with my second child and I needed a break. That morning, I received a phone call from my husband. He had realized he'd miss Mother's Day so he had rearranged his plane reservations. He was coming home a day earlier than planned and I needed to clean up the house in a hurry. I thought it was sweet of him, but there was one catch. I had picked out what I wanted for Mother's Day. It was a cute, fluffy kitten from the local, horse barn. OOPS! My husband didn't like cats. Especially house cats. He was a dog person. Time to hide the evidence.

I dropped my daughter off at the school shoeless, because she had taken them off and thrown them out of the window as we were driving to her preschool. I didn't notice they were missing, but the teacher did. My mind was elsewhere.

I arrived home and began cleaning when the phone rang.

"Hello, this is the headmaster of the Montessori school and I need to talk to Alice's mother."

"Speaking," I squeaked as I tried to hold on to the telephone while fighting with the vacuum cleaner cord.

"Alice is unhappy with her lunch."

"We've already had this argument this morning. You tell her to eat it. It isn't going to kill her and I'll give her a special treat when I pick her up. I haven't had time to get to the grocery store and so I was limited in what I could offer," I said sternly. I couldn't deal with this. I had to get the house clean, buy groceries and hide a kitten.

There was silence at the other end of the line and then headmaster said, "Exactly what did you send?"

"A ham sandwich, yogurt and…um…oh yeah … raisins!"

"I see the pack of raisins, but the rest of it looks like cat food."

I walked over to the kitchen counter and there was Alice's lunch. The kitten had come with a brown paper bag of dry cat food. I'd grabbed the wrong brown paper bag when I threw in the raisins.

"Oh my, I didn't mean to send cat food, I just got a baby kitty, and I'm sure you must be wondering why Alice doesn't have any shoes today. She threw them out of the window. I'll be right there with her lunch and another pair of shoes." I grabbed what I needed and I was off to the school.

I stopped at the first stoplight and I started to reminisce about the conversation I just had with the headmaster and I started to laugh. It hit me really hard. What must the headmaster have thought when she opened Alice's lunch, saw the cat food and listened patiently while I told her to tell my daughter to eat it? I'm sure the teacher told the Headmaster about Alice also showing up at school with no shoes. The Headmaster must have been thinking. *What is wrong with these people?*

There is nothing more awkward than laughing hysterically alone in the car with total strangers staring at you at every stoplight. I'm glad they didn't call the police, assuming I was crazy.

I composed myself by the time I reached the door of the school and I managed to slip the lunch and shoes to her classroom teacher without having to see the headmaster.

I didn't have time to do a thorough cleaning, but I had a few tricks up my sleeve. Grabbing all the dirty clothes and placing them in the guest, bathroom tub, I pulled the shower curtain closed knowing my husband would never look there. Then I acted like a bulldozer and rammed all the toys in the closet off the family room floor. He never used that closet. I opened the food I bought at the restaurant and placed it in pans so it appeared as if I'd toiled and cooked all day. I even fried up some onions as a great decoy. Then it was time to find a place to hide the kitty. My husband had never placed a foot in the laundry room. Aha! Voila!

I picked up my daughter. The house appeared clean and dinner was on the table when I heard the garage door open. My husband came in the door carrying packages and his suitcase.

"Hi, honey," I said as I gave my husband a kiss on the cheek. "What a surprise to see you home early."

"I didn't want to miss Mother's Day. I got you something special."

I wanted to change the subject quickly; I already had my *something special. Its name was Itty-Bitty-Kitty.*

We were sitting and having a great conversation during dinner when my husband looked in the direction of the laundry room. He squinted and got up from his chair and headed in that direction. I got up and followed closely behind. There under the door was a little kitten paw, going back and forth like it was trying to catch something on the other side of the door.

My husband opened the door and gruffly said, "What's this?"

"It's your daughter's new kitten. Isn't it cute?"

"It's going outside. I'm not having a cat in the house. I can't stand cats."

"It's a baby. It's freezing outside. It will die out there."

"We'll put it in the garage closet. It will be okay. It has fur."

I started to cry. Alice started to cry. My husband took the kitten out to the garage with water, cat food and an old pillow. We went to bed and I rolled over facing the other direction. I was worried that I was going to wake up to a dead kitten in the garage.

It was the middle of the night and I heard someone rumbling around in the closet. I woke up to see Bill heading downstairs with something in his arms. I got up and followed. He was heading out to the garage. When I got there, Bill was plugging in a heating pad with a special baby blanket for the kitten.

"You may appear tough, but you are a big marshmallow inside," I said as I started to laugh.

That kitten stayed outside for one night. After that, you would find that kitten sitting in my husband's lap while he read the paper, watched TV or played on the computer. So much for not liking cats!

Raising Kids in Charlotte

Missing Minnie

My mother had domestic help while she worked full time. It was unusual for a woman to work in Blooming Prairie in the early 1960's. I remember feeling so different from the other children because their moms were always home. I was embarrassed when my mother would send me with a neighbor to a special Brownie Scout ceremonial when I was honored for getting a new badge. Once, I hid in the house when I was supposed to be picked up by the neighbor. I didn't receive my badges that time.

I was never bullied about it, but I didn't want to be different. However, my family was different because we had live-in help and her name was Elena Cortinas, or to us, Helen. I don't know why we called her by the American translation; I guess that was her name in America. Helen was family to me. She wouldn't eat at the table with us. She preferred to eat in the back of the kitchen, or she'd eat later at the dining room table when everyone was finished. She slept on a twin bed in the back hall, if she spent the night. Helen attended weddings, graduations, birthday parties and all family celebrations. Her family was our family and they were friends who came to our house regularly. Helen and her daughter, Genevieve, took care of my daughter, Alice, as a baby. They called her Alice Morales. They taught her the names of her facial features in Spanish and Alice was so proud when I would pick her up and she would point to her mouth and say, "Boca."

I loved Helen. It was a handful for her at times taking care of two young kids at her age, but I knew she loved me and my younger brother Ronny very much. My older brothers were either serving in the Navy or in college. My mom and dad worked together long hours and so Helen became my pseudo mom. She was always there for me, making me tacos and tamales with macaroni and cheese. Ronny would beg for cherry pie filling and he would eat it straight out of the can. Helen would mutter Mexican slang under her breath when she would catch him eating it out of the can. Those were the days in Minnesota and my experience with house help growing up in my hometown.

In 1979, my husband announced we were moving to the Carolinas. I had to get out a map; I had no idea where we were going. *Do they have cars there?* The only Southern experience I'd had was watching Gomer Pyle on TV and

I had my doubts. People were worried for me. They weren't sure I would have running water and electricity. There was a preconceived idea about Southerners.

Coming to Charlotte, North Carolina, was such a culture shock for me. I was called a hemorrhoid. I was teased with, "If you come and go, you ain't so bad, but if you stay, you a pain in the ass!" First of all, I never heard someone use the word *ain't* in Minnesota. The locals maybe ended a sentence with a preposition like, "Would you like to go with?" However, using English poorly meant you were uneducated. That was taboo. I couldn't understand words like *tire*, *fire*, *hollow* and *power*. They sounded like *tar*, *far*, *holler* and *par*. It didn't take long before I started sounding Southern. I found that if I faked a Southern accent on the phone for a service, I would be guaranteed that the person would show up to fix my appliances. Otherwise, I was stood up a few times when I sounded like a Yankee.

So "talking funny" to the local Southerners became a norm for me. Asking where I came from and not knowing where Minnesota was located was also normal and I accepted being a hemorrhoid. I was okay with it. I'd accepted being different.

One day a neighbor asked if I could use some help cleaning the house one day a week. She informed me that the lady's name was Minnie and I would need to pick her up at SouthPark, a ten-minute drive for me. I wasn't sure

I could afford it, but I needed the help. I had a baby and a preschool child at home. I'd managed to secure work through IBM teaching English as a Second Language to their foreign workers. It was a great job and I loved working with people from all over the world. So I was thrilled to be able to bring Minnie aboard one day a week into the crazy Gruhn household to help me keep the house neat and organized.

I met Minnie for the first time and I watched in admiration as her dark eyes smiled back at me, something I had never experienced in my small town in Minnesota. When she smiled, which wasn't often, her teeth were white as snow. She didn't realize that she would become a member of the family. That is how I grew up and so I expected Minnie to understand that. She screamed and kicked all the way until she gave up and began to trust me to help her when she needed it. She agreed to take care of Alice, my daughter, for extra pay, while I went to work. Later, Jennifer, my youngest daughter, was added to her work load and she was given more pay. I don't know how she took care of two kids, cleaned, washed all of the clothes and managed to feed and entertain two little ones. Minnie was amazing. I did have problems communicating with her. She spoke a dialect called Gullah or Geechee and many times I would nod my head in agreement even though I didn't have a clue as to what she was saying. I was embarrassed to ask her to repeat what she was saying so many times. She told the neighbor she worked for that I was either deaf or stupid because she would ask me where something needed to go to be put away and all I did was nod my head up and down. Oh well, I still considered her family, which made her very uncomfortable in the beginning of the relationship.

If I didn't have to work, I would make her lunch and want her to sit at the table with me. It took her awhile, but soon she enjoyed our little lunch chats. I would ask her about her life and growing up in the South. I'd never been exposed to racism or what it was like during the Jim Crow era. I had the courage to ask her to repeat words slowly so I could learn her dialect. It was fun for me and she sensed my honest interest in her.

One night, my daughter Jennifer was asking for her "lowdy" and she wouldn't go to sleep without it. I picked up every stuffed animal, book and toy trying to figure out what a "lowdy" was. The next week, I heard Minnie say in her dialect, "Lordy (lowdy), Lordy (lowdy), where is that blanket!" Then I knew what a "lowdy" was. My daughter's name for her beloved blanket.

I would tell Minnie that if she was ever in trouble, I would help her. Sometimes she called me when she was "left" by her driver, Ida May, another maid who worked in Charlotte. A group of five women drove together to Charlotte from Van Wyck, a small town in South Carolina. Minnie was part of that group and she didn't have a car or a driver's license. It turned out that one of the ladies Minnie worked for, was late getting her to her driver. She told Minnie it was her problem how to get home and that she could sleep on a park bench. I thought that was cruel. So Minnie called me and I picked her up at SouthPark and drove her home. It wasn't the only time I drove her home. She missed her ride a couple of other times. I always had some clothes, furniture or appliances that I didn't need in the car to drop off at her house. Someone in her family was able to use it.

Minnie was respected in her small town. She helped many other families on her small income. Once I picked her up in the truck so she could drop off a sectional couch for a family. She thought that was special.

When she developed heart disease, my husband bought her medication because she didn't have enough money for the prescription. I was given a hard time by the other women who hired Minnie for "spoiling" the help. I didn't pay any attention to those ladies; they didn't like me either because I was from the North. That was one thing Minnie and I had in common, we weren't accepted as being equal in the South.

One day the neighbor called me to tell me Minnie died of a heart attack. I was shocked and I cried like a baby.

"When is the funeral?" I asked.

"You can't go. The church is black."

"What does it matter what color the church is?" I couldn't believe that a congregation painted their church black.

"You're a white person and there is separation of black and white. What's wrong with you? You can't go to that funeral. You'd be the only white person there."

"Oh." I had no idea that churches were segregated. I'd never heard of that before. We didn't do that in Minnesota. I thought back to Helen, my former Mexican nanny, who was Catholic. I knew she attended the Catholic Church, and they weren't white. Wow, I thought, we were all children of God. I didn't know he had made that distinction.

I'm going anyway. I called information and got the telephone number and the directions. A neighbor was willing to take care of my children and I was on my way to Van Wyck to attend Minnie's funeral.

I pulled into the gravel parking lot and saw Cadillacs, Lincoln Continentals and Dodge Chargers with fancy wheels and purple lights that lit up the underside of the cars. Since I was late, I slipped in a side door and sat down in an end pew. I remember the African American children turning around with their braids held together by bright plastic bows and balls. They stared at me. I still can recall their shocked little faces. *What is she doing here and who is she?* I smiled and waved at their dumbfounded little faces. Yes, I was the only white person in the church.

The choir was singing, and people were waving their hands in the air and rocking back and forth. I never saw this type of godly praise in the Lutheran church I attended at home. This was a culture shock for me, but I found it exciting and I'm sure Minnie in all her glory was amused.

All of a sudden I heard the preacher burst out, "Bring the family forward. Praise the Lord!"

The next thing I knew, the lady with the big hat and brightly colored muumuu grabbed my hand and dragged me up to the front of the church. I had no idea that I'd sat in the "family" pew. We made a horseshoe circle around the casket and I had the muumuu person on one side and a big, burly guy in a three-piece suit with an expensive hat and gold chains on the other. They raised my hands in the air and they started singing and swaying. I had no choice but to do the same. One by one each family member gave a short wail on how grateful they were for Minnie. Then it was my turn. I looked out into the congregation at those shocked little and big faces and in the same tone I wailed and praised Minnie for being my friend and loving my children. The woman next to me dropped my hand and I thought I was in trouble. She picked me up and gave me the biggest bear hug and everyone started clapping and singing. We circled the casket hand in hand singing and dancing. I'd never seen this at a Lutheran funeral in Minnesota, believe me!

I snuck out the side door when the funeral was over and jumped in my car and headed home. I gave my final blessing and I was sad knowing this would be the last visit I made to Van Wyck.

Where the Sun Don't Shine

Embarrassing? Yes. Painful? Definitely. Humiliating? No doubt about it. This was my day in the emergency room at Charlotte Memorial Hospital. It started with the birth of my second child, Jennifer. I was in the labor room screaming for my husband and the doctor with a nurse who had forty-seven minutes of experience in obstetrics. Jennifer's head started to crown and the nurse left the room to find the doctor—or doctors, I should say, since my husband happened to be one himself. There I was, all alone, with my legs crossed in an Indian style position on the labor table supporting my daughter's shoulders with my hands. All of a sudden this *slippery watermelon* landed between my legs. I'd never seen what a child looked like right after birth, much less an umbilical cord. I didn't want to scream "help" because I'd read all of these books about "delivering your child in a bathtub to prevent psychological trauma," or "singing to your child during labor and birth," or "your child knows your voice." I wanted her to have a good first impression of her momma. She would hear that screaming voice in due time. She didn't need to know it now. Well, the only difference between my birth experience in the labor room and a covered wagon on the prairie was "lights." I wiped her body with the corner of my gown and proceeded to clean her lovely, little face. I covered the umbilical cord with the other corner of my gown. It gave me the creeps. It looked alien. The doctors entered the room and the nurses had to support my husband as he almost fainted. *Excuse me. I just had a baby. Could someone help me a little, please?*

I had incurred some ruptured areas due to the fact that the position I'd birthed in didn't use the gravity method. The hospital soothed my pain with wonderful heat lamps that were placed near my private parts under a privacy sheet draped over my legs. It felt as if I'd stepped into a warm bath and the sensation brought me nearly to a hypnotic stupor. I couldn't take pain medication because I was nursing and, of course, I already knew the sacrifices of motherhood from my first child, Alice.

I was dismissed from the hospital and as soon as I arrived home, I hobbled to the closet in the laundry room to retrieve one of those heat lamps. I was already going into that stupor state anticipating the warmth of those lights. *Ahhhhhhhh.*

I placed the lights just so, covered my legs with a sheet and laid back for the forty-five minute, soothing heat session. It felt wonderful. I put the lamp back in the closet and proceeded to take care of my newborn infant. I kept feeling a funny tingling sensation between my legs, but I assumed it was the healing process taking place.

My husband returned home from work only to find me with a pack of ice between my legs and tears running down my cheeks.

"What's wrong? Why are you crying?" he said in a caring and gentle manner.

"I think I'm sunburned," I squeaked out in between gasping breaths of excruciating pain.

"Where are you burned?" He examined my arms and neck.

"Down there," I said as I pointed to my private parts.

"Let me look." He lifted my gown. "Oh my gosh, this is at least a class two burn. We have to take you to the emergency room."

"Can't you just get me a prescription for some type of cream that takes away the pain? I tried some Solarcaine and it burned in a different way."

"I'm a rheumatologist, not a dermatologist, and your stitches are stretched from the swelling. How did you do this?"

"I used the heat lamp that I found in the closet in the laundry room."

He went over to the closet, took out the light and blurted out, "You used a sun lamp. Don't you know the difference?"

"No, but I do now," I said as my whimpers grew louder.

We called the neighbor to have her stay with the children. The ride to the emergency room required a donut of ice on the seat and I held myself about one inch above it while I hung on to the seat belt. Every so often my upper arm strength would give way and I would scream when my bottom touched the ice. This made driving for my husband a little difficult.

We arrived at the emergency room with all of the tragedies and phlegm producing sounds, which made me feel like I wanted to turn around and go home. Now!

I went to the reception desk and a middle-aged, African American woman was sitting behind the counter.

"Can I help you?" she said as she peered over her reading glasses while multitasking.

"I sunburned my crotch," I whispered, hoping that the traumatized victims wouldn't hear.

"Say what?" she said as she gave me that tucked-in-chin, big-eyed look full of attitude.

"I had a baby and I mistakenly grabbed a sun lamp instead of a heat lamp to warm my private parts."

I could tell she was still processing what was wrong with me.

"Go sit down and we'll call you."

"Well, that's my problem. I can't sit and I'm getting uncomfortable holding this ice pack between my legs with my husband's underwear."

She stood up and looked at the small puddle that was increasing in size at my feet.

"Get a mop. This girl's making a mess. You incontinent, too?"

I'm sure the people in the emergency room thought I had an incontinence problem, but at this point, I didn't care. I was completely beyond humiliation.

I was whisked away and placed on a gurney with a wonderful staff that helped me out despite the giggles and whispers I heard behind the curtain. A doctor removed my stitches and gave me a topical salve that reduced the pain.

The sun lamp's new home was the garbage can. I was happy with that.

Waitress for a Day

"Can you come in and cover for one of my waitresses for today?" my brother Ty asked me in desperation on the phone. "She didn't show up."

"I've never waitressed before. I've only been the cashier," I said, waiting for my brother's *never mind* reply.

I had worked the cashier checkout at Ty's restaurant on Seventh Street and Pecan in downtown Charlotte for a couple of hours during the day. Ty needed someone he could trust at the register. I knew the bartenders and waitresses, but I had no idea what they did.

"No problem," Ty said in his strong Minnesota accent. "Thursdays are always slow and I'll be back in an hour or so after my appointment with the ABC board."

"Okay, I'll be right down," I blurted out like I was the flying nun to the rescue.

I drove the twenty minutes effortlessly with no thought as to what my future duties would entail. I arrived at the music-hall restaurant in my paisley dress with an ear-to-ear smile on my face. I knew waitresses should be friendly. I knew that well and I didn't need coaching. I was in a very good mood and willing to help out my brother.

"Here are the order tickets," Ty said. "Shorty will answer all of your questions."

"Shorty?"

"The cook," my brother yelled over his shoulder as he went out the door.

I looked around, and there was one couple sitting at a booth on the second tier of the restaurant. I took my ticket book and asked them if they wanted anything.

"More water," they replied without even glancing my way. I realized this was their cue to not bother them while they were talking.

The door opened and four more people took a table. I rushed to their side and asked them what they wanted.

"Can we see a menu first?" one of the businessmen asked with a snide look on his face.

"Oh, yeah, of course, you need a menu first." I giggled out of nervousness and stupidity.

The bell on the door rang a second time and four more people in scrubs came in and sat down. Obviously a quick lunch for them before they headed back to the hospital. I managed to get the menus to them and I heard, "Excuse me, we're in a hurry. Can we order now? We know what we want."

I pulled out my ticket book and was ready to write their order. I was so excited—this was my first time waiting on someone. I felt so important.

"I'll take a hamburger, no onions, mustard, pickles, no mayo, ketchup…."

"Wait, slow down," I said, as I was writing the order in long hand. I didn't have enough room to write the order on the first page, so I went to the next ticket to finish my dissertation.

"Excuse me," another customer interrupted, "could you clean off that dirty table so we can sit down?"

"Sure," I said to the couple that just walked in. I turned back and placed the ticket-order book on the table.

"Write down what you want. I have to go clean that table." The people looked at me a little bug-eyed and off I went.

I grabbed a tray and placed the dirty dishes and messy napkins on top. I was getting a little sick from the fumes of the garbled food when I heard, "Excuse me, can you take our order? We're in a hurry."

"Sure," I said, and I walked over to the next batch of customers and handed my dirty tray to the gentleman who was conveniently sitting on my right, while I ran back to get the ticket book that was filled out by the other group at the next table.

"Oh, I shouldn't have had you hold that tray," I said to the man as I returned. I could see the disgusted look on his face. "Sorry," I mumbled.

The bell rang again and more people walked in. It was almost a full house. I saw that the bartender was helping me take orders. *Thank God.* A man got up and was walking towards me with an angry look on his face.

"Could you bring some ketchup to our table?" he snapped.

"Get you own ketchup. I don't even wait on my husband," I snapped back as I tore off the filled out tickets with a jerk as if I were ripping the man's head off.

"Oh, and here." I handed the group at the next table the ticket book and told them to write down what they wanted. The customers were trying to hide their snickering after overhearing my snappy comment. I got the ketchup, told a man at the bar to give it to the grumpy guy requesting it and I handed the torn-off tickets to the cook.

I turned as I heard, "What's this?" Then I was hit with a couple of smashed-up, wrinkled tickets. "You aren't here to write one of your college papers!" Shorty screamed.

"I've never waitressed before," I said.

Shorty came out and gave me a quick lesson: "'K' for ketchup, 'O' for onions, etc. If they don't want it on their hamburger, don't write it down as 'no onions!'"

As I was hearing the door ring again with more customers, Shorty pointed to the cook station, "You have to get these plates out while they're still hot."

I looked around and thought, who ordered this? I didn't have a clue. I didn't know you were supposed to number the tables. The orders were coming out so fast that I had to take the plates and put them in front of customers sitting at the bar.

"Don't touch these plates. I have to figure out who ordered what," I said to the people sitting there. They looked at me like I was a cyclops. All of a sudden, I had a brilliant idea. I would figure out whose plate was whose. I put my fingers in my mouth and blew a big whistle. The room became quiet.

"Okay," I said as I put on plastic gloves, "when you recognize what I'm describing, I want you to raise your hand. Who ordered a cheeseburger with I think slaw, pickles...mayo...well...maybe not...and an order of fries?"

I saw a hand slowly creep up in the air. The person was looking side to side to see if anyone else was lifting their hand. "We have a winner," I said, running the order to her table.

Shorty stuck his head out and shouted, "Holy crap, she's running this joint like a classroom." People began eating, raising their hands to my requests and I kept bringing more food to the tables.

I ignored Shorty and I continued my classroom technique. I managed to clear the bar of all the food. Then I looked at all the dirty dishes at the tables and people waiting to sit down. I rushed to the tables with my tray, grabbing as many dishes, messy silverware and napkins as I could pile on. With the heavy tray in hand, I turned to go to the back hall to the kitchen when a plate began to slip. I tried to catch it as my toe caught the empty stools behind the cash register. I went splat on the floor, covered in dirty dishes and half-eaten food, with my body wedged behind the cash register by the wooden stools on top of me.

It seemed like a long time before anyone missed me, but eventually someone heard my pleas for help. I looked like a walking smorgasbord. People were laughing and I was totally humiliated. I went to clean the next table and I picked up a note on top of a nine-dollar tip. It read: "I have never laughed so hard, your show is amazing. We will be back tomorrow."

All I could think was, *really*?

Heather's Miracle

I was a contracted speech pathologist for a home health agency in the late 1980s and early 1990s. At that time, I'd recently attended the American Speech and Hearing Convention where I met David Muir at his exhibition booth. He was a man with cerebral palsy and he and his father were advertising his new invention, the Passy Muir device. He gave me a homemade videotape along with his phone number, in case I ever came across a patient on a ventilator who could use a Passy Muir. He had only invented devices for adults at the time. Here is my story.

The ventilator whooshed in a rhythmic beat, sustaining the frail eighteen-month-old body. Her mother was checking the gauges and hovering over her young child like an eagle protecting her nest. The living room had been transformed into a makeshift hospital ward. Pads, swabs, alcohol, syringes and suction tubes were abundant—none of these should be surrounding a baby in her crib.

"I'll need to get a little history from you before the evaluation," I quickly commented, not wanting to distract the mom's gentle routine.

"Sure," she responded in a rote manner as if she had heard this phrase many times.

"In reviewing my records, I see your baby received a live, oral, polio vaccine at ten months resulting in a fever and then full-fledged polio. Is this correct?"

"Yes," the mother responded with a long, awkward, pregnant pause. "I called the doctor that night when she had a seizure. We went to the hospital. She hasn't been home long. It was a long hospital stay. My baby is totally paralyzed except she can move her eyes. The doctors think she's brain damaged. I know you're here for a routine evaluation. Just to make me happy. Not to fill me with false hope. It's okay. I've accepted it."

Her blank stare and rehearsed conversation mimicked a bad screenplay, likely a defensive move rescuing her from her thoughts or emotions. The reality that her child would never walk, talk or play in the sandbox with other children was too much to bear.

I walked over to the sweet, little girl lying with tubes protruding from her thin frame. It was a scene that didn't match the beautiful curls and small bow framing her porcelain face. As I approached the crib, I noticed she followed my movements with her eyes for short periods of time, but her usual posture was staring straight ahead at the white, sterile ceiling, while she lay on her back.

As I was adjusting the tracheostomy, the oxygen tube protruding from her throat, I asked the child's mother, "Has anyone ever tried using a Passy Muir device on her tracheostomy to see if she can make sounds? I just met the man who created it at the American Speech and Hearing Convention in Chicago. He gave me a videotape and talked to me. I don't know if he has tubes for infants, but I can call and ask him. He gave me his phone number."

The mother stopped what she was doing and looked in my direction. Tears were welling in her eyes and she whispered in a choked manner, "Did you say she may be able to make sounds? I would be so happy if the only thing she could say was 'Ma.'"

Heather developed speech and language skills typical for her age. She was able to complete her schoolwork by operating a computer with a mouth stick. Moving her wheelchair independently and activating environmental objects required her to use a "sip and puff" method. Heather attended public school and her community church, even though she had an immune deficiency. She graduated and happily lives with her family. She smiled at my jokes and funny stories and says "Ma" all the time!

Living in Weddington

Blue Light Bandit

"Bill, look at this," I said as I pulled out the local section of the Charlotte Disturber, which was our little nickname for the local newspaper, *The Charlotte Observer.*

As usual, my husband's face was buried in the world news and he wasn't responding.

"Bill, BILL! This is important. Are you listening?"

"Uh-huh," he muttered unconsciously.

"A woman was raped by a man posing as a policeman. He used a blue light on top of his car and he pulled the woman over. It says that if you are unsure about an unmarked car, you are instructed to pull over at a gas station or in a public area. What a weirdo won't do next! Remember the man that snuck into the Mayo Clinic and posed as a doctor in an OB/GYN ward and did a full examination?"

"That wasn't a stranger. It turned out that the man was a minister and he didn't want to embarrass the woman who mistook him for a doctor."

"Oh, of course, that makes sense to me," I said with a snicker.

"Well, I've got to go, or I'll be late. Love ya," I said as a pecked my husband on the top of his head as his face was buried in his newspaper.

Singing to the radio and driving down Highway 74, I was confident I would make it in time for my 3:30 p.m. appointment at Wingate Elementary School. It was an important meeting.

I was changing lanes when I noticed an unmarked car with a blue, flashing light quickly approaching. *The Blue Light Bandit! He was following me! Oh no, I have to find a gas station. Would the Blue Light Bandit strike at three in the afternoon?* I was shaken to say the least. I proceeded to drive to the next gas station, which was about two miles ahead. I was changing lanes and playing "hard to get." He stayed on my tail. I was proud of my ability to try and outwit him.

"You scoundrel, you won't get me!" I said with full confidence. I'd worked in a criminally insane unit for ten months and I knew how to protect myself.

A few minutes went by and this guy wasn't giving up. All of a sudden, a state trooper heading in the opposite direction crossed the median and headed my way. I was thrilled that he would protect me from the Blue Light Bandit. He headed straight for me in chicken style and forced me to move to the shoulder. *Of course, he was going to have me stop and chase this imposter.* All of a sudden, two more state troopers pulled up to the side of me. *Great,*

I'm surrounded and protected from the Blue Light Bandit. Or, so I thought. Four officers approached my car with guns drawn.

"Get out and place your hands on the hood of the car!" they shouted at me. AT ME!

"What about the Blue….." I didn't even get to finish my question.

They opened my car door and grabbed my arm and pushed me down on the hood of the car.

"This car has been reported stolen from Carolina Bone and Joint. You are being charged with speeding and resisting arrest in addition to stolen property."

"What?" I screeched, hoping I wasn't mooning all of the school busses that were leaving the elementary school next to the road thirty feet from me. The same school where my appointment was scheduled.

"My husband is a physician at Carolina Bone and Joint. I didn't steal this car. We haven't transferred the title yet."

I could see that the Blue Light Bandit was talking on his phone and he motioned to one of the other officers. Obviously, this guy wasn't the Blue Light Bandit. The officer walked back to me.

"This wasn't the car stolen. Apparently it was Dr. Abda's car that was stolen."

I stood up and straightened out my suit and skirt and I proceeded to get back in the car.

"Not so fast, Ma'am," the Blue Light Bandit imposter said. "We clocked you going 57 in a 45 and the resisting arrest still sticks. We need to see your license and registration."

I plopped myself in the car with a disgusted look on my face. I handed the officer my license and proceeded to reach over to the glove compartment to get the car registration. When I opened the glove compartment, needles and syringes, lidocaine bottles, gloves, papers and finger cots dropped out on the floor.

"What's that, Ma'am?" the officer said with great interest as he pointed to the finger cots and syringes. I'm not sure if he thought he was busting a heroin addict or a prostitute.

"My husband is a rheumatologist and he uses lidocaine to numb the skin around joint injection sites. And this," I said with a smug grin as I held up a finger cot, "is not a miniature rubber. My husband rolls these on his fingers to protect himself. These are really old and now doctors use latex gloves."

I looked at the officer and he was quite embarrassed. That made two of us. I continued digging through the debris until I came upon the registration that was still in Carolina Bone and Joint's name.

"We haven't transferred the title. We just bought the car yesterday," I said as I handed it to him.

The Blue Light Bandit imposter waved the other officers to move on and he went back to his car to check my license and registration. I checked my watch and I was going to be late for my appointment. I was sure that someone had seen me sprawled on the hood. The longer I waited, the more disgusted I became. He slowly walked back.

"Here is your license and registration. You can pay these tickets or appear before the judge on this date. Sorry about..." I didn't let him get another word in.

"Oh, don't worry, I'll see you in court. I read in the newspaper about the Blue Light Bandit this morning and so when I saw your light, I panicked. You've got no idea what that does to a woman. I've been driving on this road for five years. Where's the 45 miles per hour sign you're talking about?"

"If you'd read a little further in the paper, Ma'am, they changed the speed this past week from 55 to 45 and that's why we're monitoring this road."

"Oh...well...I'll have a talk with the judge. See ya in court."

I drove to my meeting and fortunately no one saw the incident. I wasn't a felon in the eyes of my colleagues.

Four weeks went by and I arrived early at the court house for my 10:30 a.m. appointment. It was my first visit to the Union County Courthouse and I wasn't familiar with the protocol. I took a seat in the back of the courtroom as I surfed the surrounding area. I saw innocent victims and future felons in addition to lawyers, clerks and law officers. Ahh, and the Blue Light Bandit imposter was there. My appointment time was long past and I saw that I might be there for a while. I pulled my car phone out of my briefcase and out of the bag to notify my next client that I may be running a little late. I dialed the number and the next thing I knew, someone was grabbing my arm and asking me to leave the courtroom. It was an officer.

"Follow me," he said. "It's against courtroom etiquette to use a cell phone. Didn't you read the sign?" the officer said impatiently.

"Sorry, officer, I missed that. I had to call a client because the courtroom must be running a little late. I had an appointment at 10:30 a.m. to see the judge."

The officer laughed, "Do you see all of those people in there? They all have an appointment at 10:30. You'll be here all day."

"I can't. That's crazy. I have patients to see."

"Let me see your ticket."

I handed it to him.

"Resisting arrest?" he said in disbelief. I guess I didn't appear to be the type to resist arrest in my suit and pearls.

"I thought the officer was the Blue Light Bandit and so I was looking for a gas station to stop at," I said in defense.

"That's plausible. And speeding 57 in a 45?"

"Yeah, I didn't realize they had just changed the speed limit. I'll probably get nailed on that one."

"You can talk to the DA when they make that request and you can plead Improper Equipment. If you have a clean record, they'll let you off with nine miles over. Won't give you insurance points or count against your driving record. Don't tell anyone I told you that."

"What's Improper Equipment?" I asked.

"Your speedometer doesn't work properly. Some people have it tested and some people just use that plea."

"No problem. Thanks a lot and I won't use my cell phone."

I went back in and waited for them to make the announcement to approach the DA.

A clerk walked in front of the courtroom and stopped at the front of the aisle. "For those of you that would like to plead your case to the DA, you may line up here."

I jumped up and was first in line.

"Sir, I would like to approach the judge to explain the reason for my resisting arrest and my speeding ticket," I said to the DA.

"You may approach the judge."

I walked up to the judge and I was so happy to see that she was a woman. She would understand my dilemma. This was my chance to perform as the wannabe lawyer my family tried to groom me to be.

"Your Honor," I said as I sauntered toward the front of the room, "I've been charged with speeding and resisting arrest and I would like to explain to you the reasons for my behavior."

"Proceed," the judge said without acknowledging my presence. She was writing and not even looking at me.

"Well, I was speeding because I…I have a problem with…ah...ah…" I couldn't remember the name of the speedometer problem but I continued. "You know…when your thingy doesn't work."

The judge lifted her head and she had a puzzled look on her face. I decided to get creative and I lifted my index finger straight in the air and slowly let it drop down, thinking it represented my speedometer.

"We have problems with insufficient equipment. My husband needs to have it checked." Apparently, my index finger didn't appear to represent the speedometer that I thought it did and the courtroom broke out in laughter.

"Mrs. Gruhn, what are you trying to say?" the judge said as she banged her gravel to get control over the courtroom.

"I was going too fast because that thing that tells you how fast you are going doesn't work." I was so nervous that I couldn't remember the word speedometer.

"Are you trying to plead Improper Equipment?" the judge suggested.

"Yeah, that's it. What did I say?"

"Nevermind. Improper Equipment granted. Nine mile maximum. Now what about the resisting arrest?"

"Oh, that," I said as I puffed out my chest and stood a little taller. I slightly faced the courtroom audience and I took a couple of steps with my hands behind my back and my chest thrust out.

"Your Honor, I was in a state of panic. You can't imagine what was racing through my mind when I thought about the Blue Light Special. Everyone knows how that can intimidate a woman. You can understand why I was in a hurry."

I looked at the judge and again I saw a puzzled look on her face.

"Mrs. Gruhn, I'm totally confused. What does the Blue Light Special have to do with resisting arrest?"

"You know…the blue light...the rapist. He poses as a police officer." I couldn't believe the judge didn't know. *Does she not read the newspaper?*

"Mrs. Gruhn, do you mean the Blue Light Bandit? The Blue Light Special is K-Mart."

The courtroom again burst out in laughter.

"Yes, sorry, I mixed up my words. I'm a little nervous." I was so embarrassed. The judge had to use her gravel again to gain control of the courtroom.

"I had just read about it in the newspaper that morning and so when I was approached by an unmarked car with a blue light, I just assumed it was the Bandit and

I was looking for a public gas station to stop at. That was the instruction given in the newspaper."

"Officer, would you like to comment on this?" the judge said to my Blue Bandit imposter.

"I followed her for a while, Your Honor, and I had to call for backup."

"Yeah," I interrupted, "and they made me lay on the hood of the car in front of the school where I had a very important professional meeting. The police…….."

"Mrs. Gruhn, I was talking to the officer. I'll get back to you. Officer, continue."

"We had a report that a car was stolen from the office where Mrs. Gruhn's car was registered and she wasn't stopping so we thought we had identified the stolen vehicle. It was a misunderstanding."

"I'm dropping the resisting arrest charge. You may go and pay your fine of $60 to the clerk of court office for nine miles over. Next."

I gave the officer a look that said 'I showed you' and I proceeded to the office. I pulled out my checkbook and before I could fill in the amount, the cashier stopped me by saying, "I'm sorry, we only accept cash. We have an ATM on the bottom floor or you can call someone to come and pay your fine."

"You've got to be kidding. I don't have $60 cash. I'll go to the ATM." I started for the door.

"Just wait, Ma'am, you have to be escorted by a police officer," the cashier informed me.

I rolled my eyes and followed the officer, who was standing by the counter, out the door and down the three flights of stairs to the first floor. (There was a large crowd at the elevator and the officer had told me it would be faster to take the stairs.)

"I hope I can remember my pin number. I don't use ATMs very much," I said to the officer. He didn't seem to be very amused by the whole situation. I punched in my pin and I was so relieved when the $60 popped out of the bottom of the machine.

"Okay, I've got the cash."

We headed back up to the third story of the courthouse with me toting my briefcase and books. I was huffing and puffing up the stairs.

"Here is my $60 for my fine," I said to the cashier.

"Okay, and go to the end of the checkout for your court costs."

"Court costs? You mean I have to have more cash?"

"Yes, your court costs are $100," the cashier said with an evil expression on her face.

"I'm going to have to get more cash so I need my police buddy to escort me," I said. It didn't go over well with the cashier.

"Come on, let's take the stairs again. That elevator is too slow. I won't need to work out today," the officer said. At least he had a sense of humor.

I wasn't looking forward to the three-story trek down and back in my two-inch heels, but I didn't have a choice. I decided to leave my briefcase under the counter. We managed to make it to the ATM and this time I took out $200 just in case. We were headed back up the staircase when we noticed a large crowd of people coming down the stairwell.

"Stay here, let me see what's going on. I don't know why we have all of these people rushing down the staircase," the officer said with great concern as he bounded up the stairs. People parted to let him through. I waited and soon the officer reappeared.

"They've called in the bomb squad. We have a capital punishment case going on and we've been getting a lot of threats."

"Well, can I just pay my fine and get my books and briefcase that I left by the cashier?"

The look on the officer's face changed. His eyebrows arched and his eyes squinted.

"What does your briefcase look like?" he inquired.

"It's black," I said nonchalantly. "I left it under the counter. It's heavy."

"Oh, my…it's YOUR briefcase. They think your briefcase has a bomb in it. Wait…they said the briefcase was making a sound. How could that be?"

"It's probably my car phone ringing," I meekly said. Not too many people had car phones in 1995, so it was still a new phenomenon. "I'm really sorry."

The policeman bolted up the steps, taking two at a time. It was all I could do to keep up with him. He went into the cashier's office and stopped all of the commotion by halting the bomb squad from destroying my briefcase.

I paid my fine, gathered my books, and grabbed my briefcase.

"You better book it," the officer said as I headed out the door. "That judge will throw you in the clinker if she sees you."

Heels Over Head

I was on my way to a pharmaceutical meeting at a fine hotel in downtown Charlotte, North Carolina. My husband's research department was looking for new clinical trials and we were meeting with CEO's from a number of companies who were looking for venues in the area of Rheumatoid Arthritis. I was juggling my parental duties and my role as lead Clinical Coordinator. As usual, I needed to be at two places at the same time.

When I arrived at the hotel, I realized that, in my haste, I'd forgotten my purse. *No problem*, I thought, I can get some cash for parking from my husband, Bill. He's going to be at the meeting. As I was leaving, my husband handed me five dollars for the parking. I whizzed the car down the parking ramp to the attendant on duty as I was in a hurry to get to my daughter's Open House and PTA meeting.

I looked for the parking cost on the lit-up kiosk: it read 7.15.

In a fervor, I feverishly looked for change in the glove compartment, under the seats and in the console. Getting out of the car to check the trunk, I could see more cars heading to the exit. I managed to put together a number of quarters, nickels and chocolate-covered dimes that had no doubt been under the seat for a decade. Cars were now lined up behind me. The PTA meeting was starting in just a few minutes, and I was still twenty-two cents short. Sitting in his concrete box, the parking attendant reached out with his unusually short arms and carefully took my money. Because his hands were so small, it took a while for him to take all the change. He placed it on the shelf in front of him. I'd given him all the coins first, hoping to plead my case before forking over the five-dollar bill. He had counted every penny when I finally handed him the five dollars.

"Why didn't you give me this in the first place?" he asked.

"I owe $7.15," I replied, pointing to the kiosk, which now flashed 7:22.

"That's the time! You owe $4.50."

He was laughing so hard, he leaned back to take a deep breath. Then he fell off his chair and disappeared. I waited. He didn't reappear. Leaning out of my car, I peered through his window, only to see him lying on the floor next to a wheelchair. He was struggling to get up, but he didn't have the use of his legs.

My first response——as if he was a boy drowning—was to dive in. I went through my window, pulled my torso through his window, and leaned over to give him my hand. At first, he couldn't reach it because his arms were so short. I wiggled a little closer.

That's when I started to feel the cool breeze on my upper thighs. I was backing my torso a few inches out the window when my dress caught on the metal ledge just short of my derriere.

"I'm stuck. My skirt is caught on the metal piece of the window," I told him.

He giggled. "Oh my, I can't imagine what the people behind your car are thinking."

"It's not funny. Here, boost me up."

I grabbed his hands with both of mine. His biceps were large, giving me the confidence that he was strong enough to help me. As he tried to push me back out the window, my head landed on his chest, with my bare legs halfway out the window and my dress over my head.

I was stuck. He was stuck.

"Oh, my," he giggled over and over again, flapping his little arms and hands back and forth.

"Stop laughing and let's figure out how we're going to get out of this mess," I said, wondering if he could hear my words that were being muffled by my dress and slip.

Soon I heard a voice. "Are you okay in there? What's going on?"

"Help us!" I yelled, "I'm stuck. My dress is caught on the metal ledge."

I felt a tug on my dress and someone's arms around my waist. "Bend your knees and I'll let you down slowly," the kind man said.

With the grace of an elephant, I managed to wad my legs into a ball, torn dress and all, and stand up inside the parking attendant's station. The man then helped the parking attendant back into his wheelchair. As I was rearranging my hair and dress; there I was, face to face, with the CEO of the pharmaceutical company that I'd just met upstairs at the dinner party.

"Hello, we meet again," he said. I froze in disbelief and muttered something unintelligible. This wasn't the image I'd had of our next meeting. Oh no! I thought. We'll never get the research contract now.

"Thank you, I'll be on my way," I said, flipping my hair back over my shoulder as if this was a normal occurrence in my daily routine.

Driving away, I briefly looked in my rearview mirror at the line of cars waiting to pay their bill. What was on THEIR minds? I couldn't help laughing as I replayed the events in my head and envisioned the parking attendant and CEO arriving home and saying, 'You're not going to believe what happened to me at work today!'

'Oh, by the way, the CEO must have had a sense of humor. We did get the contract.

Dirty Red

It was a normal, bustling day of making coffee, cleaning up spilled cereal, driving neighborhood carpool, looking for my husband's glasses, and finding no nylons for me to wear to work. I grabbed my makeup bag, started pulling out my hair curlers and hopped in the car to make it to my nine o'clock appointment at The Union Memorial Hospital in Monroe, North Carolina, for a Modified Barium Swallow test one of my patients was undergoing. It was a twenty-five minute drive.

As I headed down my farm driveway, I heard a helicopter overhead and I figured it was the neighbor flying his new helicopter he'd built.

I wouldn't fly that thing, I thought to myself. *And he better not crash in my horse pasture. I have enough trouble with the hot-air balloons trying to land, scaring the giblets out of my horses.*

At the end of my street, I noticed a sheriff's car with its lights flashing.

Must be an accident at the bottom of the hill, I thought. I'll just go the other direction to avoid the traffic. I tried to go around the sheriff's car and he stopped me.

"Sorry, Ma'am, get back to your house. We've blocked all the roads. I can't let you out," he said in a firm but pleasant voice.

"I have an appointment at the hospital at nine this morning. I have to be there. What's the problem?"

"Sorry, Ma'am, I don't know all of the details except that I can't let you out on the road." He saw me eying my neighbor's gravel driveway. "And don't think you can go out that side drive. I'll have to come after and ticket you."

I went back to the house and called the hospital and the home health agency that had scheduled the appointment.

"Hi, Irene. You aren't going to believe this, but I can't make the appointment at the hospital because there is a policeman blocking my driveway and he won't let me out on the road."

"Uh-huh. What's the problem?" Irene asked. "Let me guess, your horses are out and you're running down the road in a belly dancing outfit with the county sheriff following you. That was your last excuse."

"No, and quit blaming my horses. That happened once and it was years ago," I said. "I don't know why they're blocking my road. The officer couldn't give me the details. I'm going to call Sharon—she's also a speech pathologist—to see if she can cover for me."

"Sure, Kathy, I can't wait to hear what story you come up with this time." She sounded frustrated as she hung up the phone. I was an experienced speech pathologist and this was an important case.

I heard the helicopter again. It sounded like it was right over my head. I looked out of the car window and saw my horses racing around my pasture. I was afraid they'd slam into the fence. I threw open the door of the car to give my neighbor a piece of my mind and an unkind gesture for terrorizing my animals. I didn't see the helicopter, but I could hear it.

As I was running to the barn, I heard a voice over a loudspeaker: "Get back in the house. Get back immediately." I looked up to see a half-dozen men hanging out of a helicopter holding what appeared to be machine guns.

"Holy sh…!" I said as I started back for the house. Then I thought, *my daughter's show pony…I can't let her get hurt!* I headed for the gate and called for my daughter's pony, Rosie. She came running and her eyes were as big as saucers. We were both out of breath.

"Get back in your house. Now! Get out of our way!" I heard again over the loudspeaker. My little Jack Russell was going crazy. He leaped in the air as if he thought he could catch the helicopter. I managed to get the pony in her stall and I ran huffing and puffing back to the house in my Rafael suit and high heels with my Jack Russell nipping at my bottom. *He's going to bite someone and it might as well be me.*

I turned on the TV and there was no news about the road block or the helicopters. I called the neighbors. No one was home. This all felt like a *Twilight Zone* experience. I called my husband.

"I can't go to work and there are helicopters flying over our house full of men with rifles," I said, panicked.

"Kathy, it's probably the police arresting some kids that are growing marijuana along the power lines. Just wait a few minutes and you'll be able to get out," he told me in a calm voice. I hung up the phone.

Duh, I didn't even think of that, I thought. It's that time of year when the plants will be high enough to see. I calmed down immediately. All of a sudden, one of the helicopters landed in my pasture. I came out on the porch to see white vans driving frantically down my drive. They parked and out jumped ten, no twenty, no…I don't know how many men in black suits with helmets, plastic face masks and guns. They had really big guns and SBI written on the backs of their suits. *Wow, the State Bureau of Investigation. This is serious.* They ran past me into my house. I followed screaming at them to explain. Some ran upstairs and some downstairs. They threw open the windows with their guns pointed towards my backyard and their eyes on their view finders. I heard bloodhounds in the background. They were coming closer and closer. A sheriff came up and my Jack Russell tried to bite him. I picked him up before he got the chance.

"What's goin' on?" I screamed.

"Calm down, Ma'am. We have a robber on the loose. He robbed a gas station on Baker Road and we chased him to Weddington Center. We caught the guy driving, but the guy in the passenger seat took off and we've tracked him here. He has a record the length of your arm and he's known as Dirty Red. He was teaching the other guy how to steal. We figure he has $10,000 on him and a gun. He's from New York."

I'm sure I looked a little funny with my mouth hanging open, my eyes wide and my face white.

"You know, Officer," I said. "We don't even lock our doors out here. I leave the keys in the car. This is farm country."

The men left my house just as fast as they'd come in and rushed to my wooded backyard. Hurricane Hugo in 1989 left the trees and creek a mess and apparently they found the man hiding behind a blown down tree stump. The SBI tried to surround him but Dirty Red bolted. No one could shoot because they would kill one of their own men. Dirty Red was fast or he hid in a hole, because the infrared helicopter and the bloodhounds couldn't track him. The bloodhounds went back and forth across my lawn a hundred times. My Jack Russell kept sneaking out of the door every chance he could, snarling while on my porch, and I kept retrieving him. He was the only one with a clue about where Dirty Red was hiding. I couldn't believe it. Dirty Red got away from the boatload of police and the helicopters.

"We'll leave a couple of sheriffs with you, but we suspect the robber is headed in that direction for Indian Trail," the sheriff said, pointing towards the power line.

"Really? A boy from the city of New York is going to brave the woods, snakes and critters? No way! He's still here. I promise. City slickers can barely deal with the cockroaches. They don't do snakes," I said.

I looked at the men who'd stayed behind. They had a few years on them and definitely a few too many donuts, but at least I wasn't alone.

"I would feel better if we could check out my barn loft. What do you think?" I asked.

I walked to the barn and they got in their police car and drove two-hundred feet.

I waited for them to get out of their car before entering the barn. They sure didn't move very fast, more like a galumph or saunter. They stood next to my hayloft ladder.

"Don't you think you better look up there?" I asked.

"Do you have a stairway up to that loft?" one asked.

"No, just a ladder. That's it." I gave them *the look*. They must have been married because they understood what *the look* meant, 'Don't make me ask again. Just do it.'

"Joe, you go up there and I'll take a look around here."

The smaller sheriff pulled himself up the ladder and the other one took out his flashlight to look around. I didn't understand the reason for the flashlight. It was the middle of the day. Maybe he would use it as a weapon. It certainly was big enough. He walked over to the stall.

"Pretty pony. It's yours?" He shined the flashlight on the pony as if he had found something. "Looks like she's pretty hot and fiery to me. I wouldn't put my kid on her."

"She has a good reason. Your helicopter almost landed on her and you had a pack of bloodhounds running around howling at the top of their lungs. I haven't checked on the other horses in the pasture. I hope they're still there," I said, growing a little impatient. A robber who was on the most wanted list had just passed through my farm and this officer was acting like he was a horse trainer.

"Well, nothing up here," the other sheriff said as he carefully stepped down the ladder.

They both walked over to the car and made a call.

"We're headin' over to Indian Trail. Nothin' for us to do here," one officer said.

"Are you crazy? You aren't leaving!"

"Ma'am, you'll be fine. Give us a call if you know of anything."

"I'm getting in my car and going to work. I'm not staying here alone."

"Oh, no, Ma'am," the sheriff with the Cool Hand Luke attitude said. "They've got all the roads blocked for two square miles. You might as well go up to the house and get you a glass of iced tea."

"I'm not staying here alone!"

"You just get that li'l dog you had beside yer, I don't think anyone will bother ya."

He had a point. My Jack Russell would be as efficient as these two. They left and in five minutes I started to pace back and forth. I headed for the house. I got in my car with my trusty dog, locked the doors and drove up and down the driveway. It wasn't the smartest thing to do, but I couldn't sit. I saw my neighbor Keith walking around with a gun and a straw hat. Now that looked safe to me.

"Keith, do you believe this?" I said as I drove up his driveway. I was inviting myself.

"What happened down at your place? There were white vans driving by here going sixty miles an hour."

"You haven't heard? We have a robber, Dirty Red. He robbed a gas station and they've tracked him to my farm. You wouldn't believe it!"

"You have to be kidding. Well, come on in and tell Ann what's going on."

I was so glad he adopted me. My Jack Russel would guard the car while I was gone. I went in, drank some tea and talked about what just happened. We laughed about the barn investigation and then I noticed a car go by.

"Oh, my, it's my cleaning lady, Dale. I'm so glad that Charlotte has its priorities right. They'd rather take a chance that the guy would carjack her than to deal with me without my cleaning lady. I better go. She may know if the roads are open."

I followed Dale down to my house and met her inside.

"Dale, what're the roads like?"

"Why, Miss Kathy, the roads are blocked all the way to the new interstate, 485. What's goin' on? They're checkin' all the cars. I told the sheriff that I needed to get here to clean your house. I told him where you lived. He said he knew of the place and he acted like he knew you and then he let me go."

After she described the guy, I told her he was one of the fellows who searched my barn. He remembered my *look* when I was told they were leaving. I'm not surprised he let her through.

"Let's rock on the porch a minute and I'll tell you the whole story. I don't care how clean the house is, I'm just so glad you're here and I'm not alone."

We rocked on the porch and I told her the story. We laughed so hard. Dale begged me to stop because she said her cheeks and stomach muscles were sore. Every so often I would yell out, "Are you hungry? Come on in for some pancakes!" We would howl every time I would offer Dirty Red something to eat. It had been hours since he'd been seen.

We cleaned the house and Dale was on her merry way. It was quiet and I made a few phone calls to my girlfriends when my husband drove into the garage.

"Bill, you will not believe this story," I said as I met him at the door.

"What story?" He paused and looked at me. "You didn't go to work today?"

"I couldn't. The roads were blocked." He gave me *the husband look*. The one that gives you time to *tell the truth or you will be in trouble look*.

"The roads are fine," he said. He wasn't sure if I wasn't trying to get out of working.

"No, really. Call Keith and Ann. They'll verify my story."

"That's okay. I know you always have a story," he said in total disbelief.

I heard a "meow" in the house, but we didn't have a house kitty. Only barn cats.

"Bill, where's that cat meow coming from?" I said as I searched around the house, figuring that maybe a cat entered the house when all of the officers were here. Of course, Bill didn't answer. He was deep in thought about something unrelated to our conversation.

"Here, kitty, kitty, kitty," I called outside in my usual barn manner that told them it was time to eat. I heard a kitty closer to my front porch. I walked around the corner and saw that the door to my crawl space was wide open with the hook lying on the ground. I screamed.

My husband came running because he thought I was dying.

"He was under our house! I told the sheriff that a New York man wasn't going to run out in the woods with all of the snakes and critters. He has to be here. They didn't believe me. I was right. He was under my porch the whole time and that is why the infrared heat cameras didn't pick him up!" I was pacing back and forth trying to figure out my next move.

My husband looked at me like I'd lost my mind. He didn't know the story and it wasn't on the local news. "What are you talking about?"

"Dirty Red. The robber. I have to call the police. Oh, wait. I have to get the rest of the horses in before they bring back the helicopter and SBI. Come with me to the barn."

"Honey, I think you've gone over the deep end. You have a good imagination and it's getting the best of you. There's no robber here and you're acting ridiculous."

I gave him *the look* and he knew it was best to play along with my wishes.

We went to the barn and I brought in the horses. As I passed my tack room, I realized the door was open. It was closed when I was here with Barney Fife earlier in the day.

"He's been in my tack room!" I screamed as I ran to the car and grabbed the Jack Russell. My husband was behind the wheel of the car reading the newspaper. He didn't even look up.

I held the Jack Russell in front of me, like a shield, and I tossed him in the tack room. *If the guy's in there he's dead meat.* I didn't hear a sound. I peered around the corner and the dog was eating the leftover crackers that Dirty Red had found in my refrigerator. Dirty Red wasn't hungry. He also had helped himself to some sodas. I guess he took me up on my hospitality I'd been offering earlier. He had probably heard me and Dale laughing on the porch. He must have thought we were too crazy to kidnap. I looked to see if anything else was missing. Sure enough, my favorite Australian raincoat and hat were missing. *That thief! He took my coat.* I called the police and told them the story. My husband thought I was a lunatic.

I got in the car and we went back to the house. I waited. The police didn't show up. It confirmed my husband's suspicions. I decided to get some milk at the store where Dirty Red had jumped out of the car and where the driver had been arrested by the police. I needed some tea, British style.

"Tell the police I'll be right back if they come. I'm going to Weddington Center to get some milk," I told my husband, who wasn't listening or answering.

I drove to Weddington Center and I ran in to get milk. Tommy and Judy were behind the cash register.

"Let me tell you what happened to me today," I said. I loved to tell stories. Judy and Tommy needed a good laugh and they were very familiar with many of my stories. They still talked about the time I drove off with the gas hose attached to my Suburban. It was memorable because I pulled the Weddington Center gas tank right off of its foundation. Gas was shooting up in the air and they had to close the station down for the rest of the day. Fortunately, my car insurance covered most of the cost and my mother-in-law covered the rest so I didn't have to tell my husband.

I continued with the Dirty Red story and when I got to the part about the coat, Tommy interrupted me.

"Wait a minute. I know that coat. That guy was in here and he bought some stuff. Used our phone and left." Judy had that wide-eyed look and I knew she had an idea.

"Tommy, let's check the security camera," she said. They had break-ins every so often and so they had finally bought a security camera. It was usually the boys on

Crane road. They would steal a loaf of bread, a jar of peanut butter and some cash whenever they came looking for money for their drug habit. They weren't violent.

We looked at the camera footage. "That's my coat. And my hat," I said.

Judy called the police and I left for the house. I was vindicated.

A few weeks went by and I went into Weddington Center to pay for my gas.

"Did you hear about Dirty Red?" Tommy asked.

"No, I haven't," I said with curiosity.

"The other guy squealed on him and they caught him in New York. He's in trouble big time," Tommy said. "You know about the phone call, don't you?"

I shook my head. "What phone call?"

"You know, the one he made here. You saw it on the security camera," Tommy said.

"Oh, yeah. What about it?"

"Turns out that he called the Yellow Cab Company to pick him up. I can't believe that a yellow cab drove thirty-five minutes out of Charlotte into the country and no one questioned it. "How many years have you lived here?" he asked.

"Ten, at least," I said.

"How many yellow cabs have you seen out here?"

I thought a minute. "None."

Tommy shook his head and Judy laughed. "Two hundred and forty-five policemen and no one questioned a yellow cab coming from Charlotte," Tommy said in between puffs on his cigarette.

"Well, I guess I can quit looking for that $10,000 in my backyard," I said.

We laughed and I giggled all the way to the car. I got in and started up the engine. Tommy came out of the store and was waving both arms at me. I waved back. I started to move the Suburban forward. I felt a jerk but I assumed it was the Suburban stalling and I gave it more gas. Oops! *Not again!*

Panic in the Pod

I was visiting St. Louis for the first time. A PBS special had talked about the architectural feat of the St. Louis Arch and I wanted to see it. It worked out that the American Speech and Hearing convention was being held there and so I decided to attend. I would be able to get credit for my license and see the Arch at the same time. I talked a colleague into attending with me, but she wasn't too interested in the seeing the Arch. On the day I wanted to tour the Arch, my friend attended a special meeting at the convention and she wasn't able to go with me. As far as I was concerned, touring alone was creepy. Alas, I ran into my professors from Appalachian State University and they invited me to tag along with them to see the St. Louis Arch. I was flattered—after all, these guys were now the hot shots of the speech pathology field and it made me feel a little bit important.

We arrived at the Arch only to have to wait one hour in line. That was fine. The professors and I were catching up on "who was who" and "what was what" and the new direction that everyone was going. They treated me with respect and as an equal. It felt good.

When we reached the end of the line, we were escorted to a little elevator that looked like a large egg. There were six of us and the single elevator only fit five. I was polite and let my friends stay together. I would go in the next elevator. As I watched people enter the small, round elevator, I didn't like the looks of it. It resembled one of those carney rides.

Plus, I'm a little claustrophobic. I wasn't always that way. But when I was 21, I got trapped in the bottom of an old submarine that had sunk in the 1900s in Lake Superior. I was wreck diving for the National History Museum of Minneapolis. I was found in the submarine right before my air ran out, after I'd taken my knife and pounded SOS on the metal inside the ship. Another diver had to provide me air out of his tank so I could "buddy breathe" my way to the top. That was the official end to the days when I had no fear, or maybe no sense.

When it was my turn to enter the elevator, the guide ushered me into the dimly lit, egg-shaped elevator and told me to take the single seat in the back. My head hit the ceiling as I entered. Four Japanese businessmen walked in behind me and sat in pairs across from each other right in front of me. Our knees were touching and it was cramped—to say the least. The men were polite, but I could tell they didn't feel comfortable with my knees touching theirs.

They scrunched closer to the elevator opening. The entrance was wide open and I was okay with this ride ahead of me. Or so I thought. The announcement came that we were departing and the door closed. Only a small porthole on the door provided an outlet for me to view the outside world.

I could feel my heart start beating faster and I was beginning to feel faint. I started to fan my hand in front of my face, but it wasn't helping. The Japanese men were busy speaking to one another and ignoring me completely. I couldn't understand anything they were saying. I felt warmer and my heart beat even faster. Perspiration was dripping off of my face and palms. I started to sing to myself with a song I learned in Girl Scouts.

"Glow little glow worm…glimmer…glimmer
Shine little thorn mate…thinner…thinner"

It wasn't working. I didn't feel comfortable so I tapped the shoulder of the man on my right who was closest to the door and asked him to exchange places with me.

"Can I sit where you are sitting, please?"

"No speak English."

I pointed to my seat and then pointed to his seat, which really appeared as if I was pointing to my body and asking to sit on his lap. He stopped talking and he had the "deer in the headlight" look. His three other friends also stopped talking and the elevator became very quiet. The poor man obviously didn't understand what I was trying to convey. The men just gave me a strange look and then they went back to their conversation.

All of a sudden, the elevator made a correction for the curve of the arch and I almost jumped out of my skin. My heart was pounding and I felt like I might explode. I couldn't stand it any longer and I dove for the porthole. I was lying across the laps of all four men and they held up their arms like they were under arrest.

"I'm sorry…I'm sorry…I'm claustrophobic," I said, and I began to sing louder.

"GLOW, LITTLE GLOW WORM…GLIMMER …GLIMMER…."

All was quiet but for me singing at the top of my lungs with my face plastered against the porthole.

"SHINE, LITTLE THORN MATE THINNER….THINNER…

"YOUR TEETH ARE FALSE AND YOUR HAIR IS PEROXIDE…

"SEE BY THE MOON THAT YOUR EYES ARE CROSS-EYED…."

I was calming down and the singing was working. Until the elevator made another correction. Oh, no, here we go again!

"PETTICOATS SWAYING IN THE BREEZES…

"SOUNDS LIKE SANDPAPER SCRAPING ON YOUR KNEESES…

THAT'S MY GIRL, DEAR BOYS AND GIRLS…OH THAT'S MY GIRL!"

Finally, we reached the top and the elevator stopped. The door opened and there were the four Japanese wives waiting for their husbands in addition to my distinguished professors. I had to crawl out face-first wiggling across the laps of those four Japanese men and landing on the palms of my hands. I was too relieved to be embarrassed. I could've kissed the floor. *Wide open spaces.*

My professors didn't say anything because they were busy in conversation and didn't witness my awkwardness. As we were leaving, I could hear in the background the Japanese wives pitching a fit. They were pointing at me and from the looks on their faces it appeared as though they were demanding an explanation. The poor men kept shaking their heads and shrugging their shoulders. I wish I'd known Japanese. I would have explained the situation, but I'm not so sure the wives would have believed me. I hope it didn't look like I wanted to be spanked. Well, I guess it did look that way.

Enjoying Retirement

Bargain Basement Burial

The phone rang and I grabbed it with a quick, "Hello?"

"Grandma has passed," Holly said, and then her voice trailed off into a whisper. "What do I do?"

"I'm so sorry," my voice cracked. "Call the funeral director; he'll guide you through it. Are you okay?" I said, looking at the ceiling hoping the tears would reabsorb in my lower lids. I loved my mother-in-law, Grandma Maxine, but I knew she had a bad heart. I wasn't so sure my sister-in-law, Holly, would be able to handle Maxine's passing, but she seemed like she was on top of things.

"How did she pass?" I asked with hesitation.

"She was quietly lying in bed looking at her rose garden through her bedroom window when she said she wanted to rest awhile. I checked on her a little later and she wasn't breathing. It was very peaceful," Holly responded.

"Just like Grandma. Sweet, quiet and no trouble," I said with a sigh.

I drove to Charlotte Memorial Hospital where my husband, Bill, worked and told him that his mother had died. Maxine had suffered from heart trouble for years and she'd endured many trips to the emergency room. We made arrangements to fly to California from North Carolina for Maxine's funeral with two children in tow. I would stay in the background and act as family support for my husband and sister-in-law, Holly. I would also be the referee because bad blood had surfaced between the two for many years.

When we arrived, there was a lot of commotion at Grandma's house. Neighbors were bringing food, the grandkids were running around and the phone was constantly ringing. It made my husband uneasy. He liked quiet and solitude; however, it was nice to know that Grandma was well loved. I tried to be the household secretary to give Bill and Holly time to organize their thoughts, but then I received a disturbing call from the funeral director.

"Hello, this is Discount Funeral Services. Is this the home of Holly Gruhn?"

"Yes, may I take a message?" I said, still pondering the word *discount.*

"We haven't received the casket and we need it now. Holly was told in advance that she was responsible for getting the casket to me. I'm a one-man business and I need to answer the phone, besides fixing up Grandma."

"Casket? Don't you have caskets?"

"No, you're to go to the warehouse, pick it out and bring it here," the director snapped.

"Bring it there?" I couldn't believe what I was hearing. "How?"

"What do you think rental trucks are for? Do you want me to give you the address?" he said in a huff.

"That would be helpful and I need your phone number and address." I couldn't believe I was having this conversation. I hung up the phone and I cornered Holly in the back bedroom. I was looking for answers.

"We're going to save over $5,000 using this discount funeral home. Mom would be proud to know I saved that much money. Dad's funeral was so expensive," she added.

"Did you know we have to go get the casket and bring it to the home?"

"Oh, I do remember something about that. I don't know how to drive a big truck. What are we going to do?"

"Get in the car. I know how to drive a truck and hurry. I don't want Bill to know we have to get the casket and that we're working with a discount funeral home. Really, Holly? Mom could afford a nice funeral."

"Mom was frugal and I was just carrying out her wishes."

"Okay. As they say, 'go with the flow,'" I said. I could tell Holly was getting defensive.

We managed to find a nice casket at the warehouse, which was not in the best part of Riverside, California. They loaded it in the U-Haul and I was on my way to the funeral home with my makeshift map in hand.

"Wow, I'm glad you're driving this truck. I would've taken out a number of cars and obstacles by now," Holly said.

I felt she was buttering me up and it was working. We pulled up to the discount funeral home. It wasn't difficult to find because it was one of the few businesses that wasn't boarded up and closed. It was located in a somewhat abandoned shopping center. A sign spray painted on the door read "Discount Funerals," but a few of the letters were smudged. I struggled to open the door as the iron guardrails encompassing it made it heavy. *Do these people really believe that someone would try to rob this place?* The only things in the room were a telephone, sitting on a metal desk with a bent leg, and a year-old calendar nailed to a chalkboard hanging behind it. Some plastic flowers served as the only wall decorations and it looked like they hadn't been cleaned in years. In front of the phone was a sign that read, "Cash only."

"Oh, my!" Holly said. "I'm glad Mom isn't here to see this."

I just rolled my eyes and managed to find the funeral director. He was wearing sunglasses, a gold necklace and a Hawaiian shirt. I was hoping he wouldn't wear that to the cemetery, but after the conversation we'd had, I wouldn't put it past him. His name was Eddie. No last name. Just Eddie. He came outside to help us remove the casket from the truck. We each grabbed a handle and we carried the casket inside.

"Much easier this time around. I thought you were going to drop your mom when we carried her out to the hearse in her bed sheets," the guy muttered to Holly.

I almost dropped my side of the casket. Holly was waving her hand from side to side as if it wasn't anything.

"It was a piece of cake," she said.

"Speaking of cake, have you made arrangements for the food?" I asked the funeral director.

"Do I look like a cook? Food? Hell, I can arrange something from one of the fast-food joints around here. The one across the street was closed down by the health department, but there's another one down the block," he said.

"No, thanks. We can handle it." I didn't need to have the people at the church die of food poisoning.

"Does the church have a women's circle?" I asked Holly.

"Yes. I'll get them on the phone and see what they can do," she said.

As we were leaving, I noticed a silver-spray-painted hearse. *This has to be a joke.* "Look," I said as I pointed to the vehicle.

"Yes, that's what he used to pick up Grandma," Holly said. "The good hearse is in the shop being fixed. Hopefully, it'll be ready for the funeral."

I couldn't believe my eyes or ears. We arrived home and the phone rang. It was the funeral director.

"Where's the death certificate?" he asked.

"You don't have it? Holly probably forgot to give it to you. I'm sure it was quite a workout hauling Grandma to the hearse and to remember the death certificate would've been over the top," I said sarcastically. "Wait a minute. I'll get Holly."

"Holly, we need the death certificate to give to the funeral director," I said as I was dealing with one disaster after another. *How could this funeral director leave without the death certificate?* It was beyond me.

"Death certificate? What's that?" Holly answered.

"It's the piece of paper that declared Grandma was dead. Was it the ambulance team or a coroner that was here who filled it out?" I asked.

"You told me to call the funeral director. I didn't call an ambulance or a coroner. The funeral director and I wrapped Mom in her bed sheet and carried her to the silver hearse. Then they took her away. You didn't tell me I had to call an ambulance."

I was still having trouble envisioning Holly and the funeral director carrying Grandma out of the house in a sheet. No gurney? Holly is a wimp and Grandma wasn't exactly a lightweight. I hope the neighbors hadn't seen anything.

"You've got to be kidding. You didn't call an ambulance or coroner? Oh no," I groaned.

"Is that a problem?" Holly asked with her typical *faraway look in her eyes.*

"Problem? You better believe it's a problem. A person has to be pronounced dead by someone authorized to do so. It's against the law to just bury someone without an authorized person pronouncing her dead. I'll call the funeral director immediately before they embalm her."

I called the discount funeral director back only to learn that Grandma had been embalmed. "Who pronounced her dead?" the funeral director sputtered in his chain-smoking voice.

"We're searching for it as I speak. Holly has it. It's here. I'll get it to you," I said, holding my crossed fingers behind my back.

"You know it's illegal to bury someone without an authorized person pronouncing the victim dead," Eddie said.

Victim? Yes, this may be a crime scene, also. I was getting some insight into the type of clients Eddie was used to working with. This was out of my control. I'd have to tell my husband that we were in big trouble. *Poor Bill. He was really trying hard to be nice to Holly. This was going to throw him over the edge. I'd better go buy a referee shirt and a whistle.*

"What?" my mild-mannered husband screamed. "I know I'm a doctor, but I can't fill out my mother's death certificate. I'm not licensed in California and it wouldn't be legal anyway. I can't pronounce her dead. Where's Holly? I've got to have a word with her."

"Hold on. Hold on. Let's not fly off the handle. I've got an idea. Are there any medical residents that you know from your college days in California that could fill out a death certificate?" I asked.

"I can't call someone I haven't seen in twenty years and ask them to do that."

"Get out your address book. You and Holly won't look good in an orange jumpsuit. We don't have a choice." I wasn't in the mood to argue and we were in a time crunch.

Bill talked an old colleague into signing a death certificate and he was off to Los Angeles to pick it up. I would've liked to have been a fly on the wall for that conversation. He had a two-hour drive and he'd arrive home just in time to pick us up and take us to the cemetery. I would hold down the fort at the house. Or so I thought.

"We have to put together food, flowers, programs and a picture of Mom for the memorial service at the church after the burial. We'd better get going. We don't have much time," Holly said matter-of-factly.

"What? We have to do that in less than two hours? Are you kidding? Have the food and flowers been ordered?" I asked as I looked at Holly's blank face. "I think I know the answer. Never mind." I was trying to keep my temper under control.

I was trying to figure out what the discount funeral home was doing, but I realized I didn't have time to think about it or, better yet, didn't want to think about it. We managed to get flowers from a local shop on the way to Kinkos. I talked the lady behind the counter into letting me use her computer to type up the program. She reluctantly agreed. We had them printed in record time and we were off to the church. The church circle ladies had agreed to organize and serve the food I picked up at the grocery store.

I'd grabbed a head shot of Grandma Maxine and placed it in a 10 by 12 frame before we left the house. I placed the two vases of white roses and the picture on a table at the front of the church. I had everything under control. Holly greeted friends and church members. That was one thing she did well. She was able to get a ride to her own car carrying the spray of roses that would go on Maxine's casket. I drove the rental truck back to the U-

Haul store and picked up the car. I had just enough time to drive home and get everyone dressed. The memorial service would take place immediately after the private burial. It looked like we had pulled it off and Bill wouldn't be subjected to any more drama.

Bill was driving with me and our daughters, Alice and Jennifer, in the backseat. We were on our way to the cemetery and I was telling them the story of the silver-spray-painted hearse when, all of a sudden, on the other side of the freeway going the other direction, we saw a wrecker hauling a silver-spray-painted hearse.

"Grandma!" everyone screamed simultaneously.

Bill was trying to cross over six lanes to get to the exit in order to follow the hearse.

"Wait, wait a minute," I said as I was collecting my wits. "Surely a wrecker wouldn't haul a hearse with a body in it."

"What if they are? Grandma may fall out the back doors," Bill said, swerving through traffic as cars were honking and people were giving us unkind gestures.

"No, no. I say we go to the cemetery first," I said, hoping I'd be right.

We arrived at the cemetery just in time as the minister approached the casket. I didn't know if we were lucky or if maybe the discount funeral home had had this experience in the past. There was another spray-painted hearse behind the tree strip. This one was painted black.

Obviously, Eddie switched vehicles. I wondered what people thought as they passed the hearses on the freeway. One of his friends had bailed him out and brought the other car. His friend stood by the black hearse in his muscle shirt, gold chains and tie-dyed pants smoking a cigarette. It didn't matter; the weather was beautiful and the array of roses covering Maxine's casket was very fitting for a woman who had a Shakespearean garden full of her own gorgeous roses at home.

Holly sauntered by and whispered in my ear, "You wouldn't believe what happened to the hearse."

"I think I have a clue," I said as the minister started to speak.

Ticking Ticket

"Hello, is this Kathy Thorson Gruhn?" the caller asked in a thick Minnesota accent.

"Yes, speaking," I said, wondering how much money this person needed for their future fund-raiser. I'd been getting a lot of these calls.

"I want to congratulate you for receiving the Distinguished Service Alumni Award from your hometown, Blooming Prairie, Minnesota. The banquet is January 26th and I hope you can come. Oh, yeah, you'll get to ride on the back of a convertible for the 4th of July parade. Isn't that exciting? Oh, this is Joanna and you probably remember my dad, Jeff Zweiner."

"Yes, the Zweiners," I repeated, trying to jog my memory from forty-three years ago.

"You'll be getting the newsletter and it will explain more. Again, congratulations."

I hung up the phone and I found *Blossoms Forever*, the Blooming Prairie Alumni newsletter from a few months ago. Featured there was the picture of the previous winner of the Distinguished Service Award, Bob Ackerwold. He had to be at least seventy or eighty years old. *I'm not that old. What did I do that I'm getting an award? I better call her back and ask her. Maybe it'll explain why in the newsletter. I'll wait.*

My son-in-law was coming to spend the night with ten of his students from Asheville, North Carolina. They had to present at a conference in Charlotte and they were happy sleeping on couches and floors. While I was waiting for them, I was busy writing a book proposal. I couldn't get the computer to work properly for filling out one of the forms and so I figured I would print it and fill it out by hand. My handwriting was so sloppy that I managed to find my old typewriter and planned to fill in the blanks using that. I hadn't laid eyes on that Brother typewriter for over fifteen years. Yup, it needed a new cartridge. I looked at the clock and it was 8:30 p.m. If I hurried, I could make it to Staples and back before the crew arrived at my house.

I grabbed the typewriter and placed it in the back seat, in case I needed it, and was on my way. I was driving down the hill and almost to the stoplight when the light turned yellow. I gunned the car and made it through the intersection right when the light flashed red. I made it. Well, so I thought. The blue lights and siren were right on my tail. How dumb. I had a police car behind me. I pulled over to an abandoned road while the policeman with beaming search lights pulled behind me. I waited about a minute and I thought maybe I was supposed to get out of my car and go to his car. It had been many years since I'd been pulled over. I forgot the protocol. I opened my door and was using my finger to point to him and then to me. Nothing happened. Well, nothing happened with the police car behind me. It was the second police car that pulled up with bright shining lights that pinned me in on the side of my car and then the third police car on the other side of me. *Wow, there must be a convict loose out in the woods next to this road.* I jumped back into the car and locked the door to be safe. One of the policemen approached my car. The other police cars surrounded me and made sure I couldn't get away.

"Give me your license. Hands on the wheel. Do you own this car?" the policeman shouted.

I was confused at first because I couldn't figure out how to get my license and keep my hands on the wheel at the same time. I decided to give them my license first, which meant rolling down the window, handing it to them and finally placing my hands on the wheel. "Yes, I own the car," I said in a squeaky voice through the partially opened window.

"What was your hurry?" the police officer again shouted.

"I need a typewriter cartridge and the store is about to close."

"Did you say typewriter?" the other officer asked. He shined his two-foot flash light around the inside of my car and stopped at the typewriter in the back seat.

"Frank, you won't believe this. This lady has a typewriter in the back seat of her car."

The other officer came over and said, "Wow, I've never seen a typewriter before." He appeared to be in his early twenties.

"Why do you have a typewriter in your back seat?" the first officer asked in the typical Dragnet style.

"I'm an author…."

Before I could finish my sentence, the second officer said, "Wow, an author that types on a typewriter. Like Hemingway or something. I've never pulled over an author before."

"Ma'am, the next time a policeman pulls you over, don't try to get out of the car. That's what people do when they steal a car or they try to run. That's why I called for backup," said the officer who was holding the oversized flashlight.

I thought about this statement and then I saw my son-in-law's van go by with all of his students inside. Here I was, lit up like a Christmas tree alongside the road with flashing lights and surrounded by police. I had to get home fast. Playing the "I'm old" card seemed to be working and so I hammed it up a little.

"Well, my reflexes are a little shaky at my age. I'll pay closer attention next time I see a yellow light," I said, hoping they would show me a little mercy. After all, I was sixty years old, but I still rode horses and jumped fences. *I'm frisky!*

The officer had turned off the glaring light and he crouched down so we were eye to eye. "I'm going to just give you a warning. So, be careful. Okay?"

"Of course, Sir," I said with a beaming smile. "Thank you."

The cars pulled away just as fast as they had appeared. Staples would be closed by now. I turned around and drove home. My son-in-law and the gang were already in my house when I pulled up. They had read the note on the door instructing them to come in.

"Sorry I'm late," I said to them.

"Oh, we understand. There was a lot of commotion on the road and the traffic was bad. Someone was really in trouble. There were three cop cars and they had this person blocked in. Must be a drug bust or something," one of the students said with wide eyes and I could tell he was glad it wasn't him.

"Oh, that was me," I said as I saw the shocked look on my son-in-law's face.

"Wow, what happened?" my son-in-law asked.

"I ran a red light hurrying to the store to get a typewriter cartridge."

"What's a typewriter cartridge?" one of his students asked.

I looked at him and a thought occurred to me: *Maybe I'm old enough to get the Distinguished Alumni Service Award.*

Training Bill

"Ronny, I want to go to the family reunion in Glasgow, Montana, with Bill. Are you up for it?" I asked my brother, hoping he would say yes and we could stay in his camper. I wanted Bill, my husband, to experience my roots on my mother's side of the family. Also, I thought we could sneak in a quick trip to Glacier National Park, one of my favorite places.

"Sure, but my truck has only one seat. That may be a stretch, driving from Minnesota to Montana with three adults in the front seat," Ronny said with hesitation in his voice. I'm not sure if he was worried about the three of us in close quarters or about a husband and wife in close quarters. It was a toss-up.

"How about if Bill and I take a train and we meet you in Glasgow?" I said to my brother.

"That sounds great!" Ronny answered. "Let's plan on it."

"Could we sneak in Glacier National Park?" I asked my brother, not wanting to push the envelope too far.

"You know that's on the other side of Montana from the family reunion," Ronny responded, again with some concern in his voice.

"How about if you and I drive the truck and camper and we put Bill on the train and meet him in Glacier."

"That'll work. Will Bill mind riding the train alone?"

"Are you kidding? After the family reunion and the fact he'll have to hear my same jokes and stories, he'll be glad to have a break. He'll be ready for round two of family after some quiet and solitude if you know what I mean."

"Yeah," Ronny chuckled. He knew his sister and brother-in-law well.

Bill and I left Minneapolis, Minnesota, on the train and we met Ronny at the family reunion in Glasgow. We had a great time reminiscing about the past. Bill heard many family stories, including the time I sank Uncle Cal's brand new truck in Porky Pine Creek. It was a good thing he didn't hear that story before we were married.

As we were putting Bill on the train with just a ticket in hand he said, "I left my billfold in the camper."

"Don't worry. We will pick you up at your stop. Our driving time is less than your train ride. We don't have time to run back to the camper." I said. Ronny and I had a six-hour truck ride and Bill had a seven-hour train ride. Perfect.

Ronny and I made it to the East Side of Glacier National Park, the small town of Polson, on Sunday afternoon. We made it in plenty of time to meet Bill. The depot seemed to be the only structure in town. It was closed for business, but the building was open.

We soon saw the train coming down the tracks and we were so happy with how the trip was panning out. What great plans we'd made. Just short of patting each other on the back. We watched the few passengers leave the train. No Bill. I started to approach one of the porters standing next to the train steps when he jumped back in and the train started moving down the tracks. The next picture I saw wasn't pleasant—my husband standing in front of a closed train door, pounding on the window, screaming, "Stop the train." I couldn't hear it, but I knew what he was saying by reading his lips.

I turned and looked at my brother and in unison we said, "Oh, no." With a definite Minnesota accent stretching out the "o."

We were in the boonies with no cell phone service. It didn't matter; my husband didn't have a phone. I ran into the station and I tried to find someone to ask when and where the next stop was. Everyone was gone. I looked on a train station schedule and saw that the next stop would be Whitefish, on the west side of Glacier Park. We took a wild guess that maybe we could make it in time to meet my husband. I was hoping Bill would have the sense to get off there. We weren't sure how long it would take for us to go through mountains with a truck and camper, but we didn't have a choice. We had to find my husband. The next stop after Whitefish was Spokane, Washington. Days away. He had no ticket, no cash, no credit card and no luggage. What a mess!

It's a mountainous drive in the Rockies. Switchbacks, steep climbs. It wasn't the type of terrain you would want two nervous family members driving through with a truck and camper at maximum speed. I'm sure people thought we were crazy drivers. The most difficult distraction was the laughter and stories. Every time it became a little quiet, I'd look at my brother and when he'd turn to look at me, I'd say, *"Oh, no"* with an exaggerated facial expression and we'd get the giggles. Sometimes I would pantomime pounding a window with my fists and yell, "*Stop the train,*" and the seat would jiggle with our laughter. Then the stories started.

"What if he gets off the train and we aren't there and he starts wandering through Glacier National Park? It could be years before we found him," I said. Ronny would laugh and I would continue.

"I would have to put pictures on milk cartons or nail flyers to the trees in Glacier…with updated photos of him with long hair, a bushy beard and a faraway look in his eye."

Each time I would end the fictitious stories with "*Oh, no.*" The laughter would begin again. It was the type of laugh where we would make funny noises. Squeaky breathing, snorts and gasps for breaths. I couldn't talk. I would shake my head *NO* and mouth *STOP* because my cheeks were sore and my tummy was hurting. It helped to relieve the stress of not knowing what would happen next.

We arrived in West Glacier and I jumped out of the truck and ran into the train station. I'm not so sure people didn't think the vehicle was on fire with the burned-rubber smell emanating from the over-worked truck. We saw the train coming down the tracks and had that déjà vu feeling. As the cars pulled into the station, we saw my husband in the window and the train stopped. Bill was so happy to see us; he had the same look you get from your kindergartner when picked up from the first day of school.

My brother turned to me and said, "Next time, you need to pin a note on his coat with his name and which train stop."

I added, "I'll make sure it's the coat with the mittens that are strung through the sleeves."

When my husband walked up I asked, "Were you reading or taking a nap?"

He snapped back. "The ticket says East Glacier and they announced the stop as Polson. By the time I saw you, the train was pulling away. I was wondering what was going to happen?"

We lost one day at Glacier Park, but we gained years of laughter. All I had to do at a family gathering was to make sure my husband wasn't looking and look at my brother, pantomime pounding on a glass door, mouthing the words *stop the train!*

Duct, Duct, Boots

Life was good. I had just returned from Weight Watchers with the crown still on my head and I was basking in the glory of having lost twenty-five pounds. I was so wound up from having sprinkled "you can do it, too" fairy dust on all the other partners in crime that I still had the energy to plan my horseback riding clinic for the next day. I pulled out my jodhpurs that would now display 20 percent less cellulite and I looked around for my full-length riding boots. This clinic required formal attire. I spied an old box in the back of my closet. As I tugged and battled the wire hangers, I realized that it contained my Vogel boots that my husband bought me years ago. There wasn't a clinic or horse show good enough for my boots at that time. Child number two came along with a few extra pounds and I had no idea that you gained weight in your legs. However, my recent weight loss had shaved inches from my calves. I'd never worn the boots. *No time like the present.*

I put my arm inside the soft calf leather and I stroked the boot like I was petting a soft puppy. I marveled at the fine stitching and tailored style. These were expensive boots and they would be worth a fortune now. Yes, the time was right to remove the boots from their shrine. Hey, I lost the weight and I wore the crown. I'll look good even if my riding is a little rusty.

I woke up early the next day with the sun shining and the birds chirping. The riding clinic consisted of a dressage and show jumping lesson with an Olympic caliber instructor, Bill Hoos. I needed to get my horse prepared, clean my tack and load everything in the trailer with a twenty-minute drive to Up and Over horse farm. I was so excited that I wasn't sure whether the hair on my legs had caught on fire because I pulled up my jodhpurs so fast. I had three hours until my lesson, but I wanted to put on my new boots and feel that soft calf leather next to my skin.

I found my boot pulls, and to make sure that I didn't accidentally scratch the boots, I covered the T at the top and the curved metal J that slips into the leather pull inside the boot with moleskin. I was ready. I put my greased and talcum-powdered left leg and foot into the boot. I tugged and pulled and my boot was on. I walked around, pretending to be Queen Camilla, with my fancy, beautiful boot.

Then I took the wrapped boot pulls and started with my right greased and powdered leg and foot. I tugged and tugged. I added a little more talcum powder. It wouldn't go on. I figured it was getting warm and my calf was a little swollen from the heat and from walking around. I removed the partially on boot and I wrapped bags of frozen peas around my calf. I placed pillows on the couch so my leg would be elevated and all the blood would go back to my heart. This was working. I wiped my leg and greased it with a good coating of talcum powder. I grabbed the boot pulls. Yes! My boot was on except for the top two-inch portion at my calf. All of a sudden, the moleskin on the boot pull slipped and came out of the boot. No problem, I would slip it back in.

Or so I thought. My boot was so tight that I couldn't slip the pulls back in. My calf started throbbing and my foot was going numb. I thought that I better get the boot jack and remove the boot and start over again. The boot jack was placed just right and I put the heel of my boot on the front of the jack to give myself a little leverage. Because of the grease and talcum powder, the boot kept slipping out of the boot jack. I knew how to solve that problem—more moleskin wrapped around the boot for good measure. I secured the boot to the jack with duct tape. Every horse owner has a handy roll of duct tape. Again I tried to get the boot off. It wouldn't budge. I looked at the clock. Only two hours before my clinic. I needed to load my horse and all my stuff and be warmed up in the arena. I panicked. By this time my leg was totally numb. *What do I do? Call 911 for a stuck boot? Go to the emergency room? NO, they will cut the boot off. Never!*

I was hopping around trying to think of what would work. Could I possibly tie the boot to the dog collar and send him out the door just when a squirrel was running across the yard? My mind was racing. I called the neighbors. No one was home. I called my husband at work to see if he had any suggestions. He said, "Just cut the boot off and have it stitched again." He was right. I went to the drawer and took out the box cutter, but I just couldn't do it. Then I had a better idea. I just needed a little more "oomph." So I took the boot jack that was duct taped to my boot and I sat on my bar stool and duct taped the boot to the bar. I slowly and carefully removed my body from the stool and hung upside down to encourage the boot to release with a little more body weight on the other end.

I guess it had been awhile since I'd taken a physics class or, better yet, a gymnastics class. I was stuck. I was hanging from my bar with my boot duct taped to the counter with the phone in sight, but I couldn't reach it. The phone rang. I tried to throw the bar stool next to me at the phone so I could get help. I don't know why I thought I was Brunhilda; I only knocked myself in the head with the legs of the stool. I finally pushed my other foot up against the bar and I wiggled and wiggled until I fell to the floor in total relief. The boot was off. The boot was attached to the bar, but I only had one hour to make it to my lesson.

Of course, I was late to the clinic and very embarrassed. There I was wearing my old paddock boots with the worn out stitching from my defunct bunions, hair plastered to my head from my one-hour boot aerobics class, a face still flushed and discombobulated as I was trying to tack up my horse.

My girlfriend Christie stopped to watch my lesson and said, " I'm a little confused. There is a beautiful Vogel boot taped to your kitchen bar. What's the story?"

Everyone looked at me expecting an explanation or better yet a story. I started out, "You won't believe this…." All I saw was nodding heads and snide looks. I think they had heard me start a story like this before.

The boots are back in the shrine.

About the Author

Kathryn Thorson Gruhn grew up in the small town of Blooming Prairie in southern Minnesota. She moved to the South with her husband in the late seventies and currently lives on a horse farm in Tryon, North Carolina. She has two grown daughters and two grandchildren.

Before becoming a writer, she was a speech pathologist for 35 years, working primarily with children ages birth to seven, which prompted her to create the *My Baby Compass* program. *My Baby Compass* is a program for parents and caregivers of children Birth to Seven that promotes the early identification of developmental delays. She recently entered in a joint venture to get *My Baby Compass* evidence-based and into an App that will be available worldwide. For more information, visit www.mybabycompass.com.

She is a bestselling author with the first edition, *Soul for Success*, and she also received the Editor's choice award.

She has been telling funny stories for many years and was finally prompted by Jack Canfield, the *Chicken Soup of the Soul* creator, to gather them in a book after he learned that writing them down was one way she handled the grief of losing her husband of forty-three years. Her greatest gift is making people laugh through her stories and jokes. Follow her at: kathythorsongruhn.com for more books and stories.

Acknowledgements

I would like to thank my family for their encouragement and help. My brother Ty and my daughter Jennifer read through the book and fixed commas and content. My daughter Alice was patient when I couldn't take care of the grandkids at the last minute because of "book stuff". Most of all, I'm glad that my family isn't embarrassed by any of the stories about me or them. I guess they are finally numb!

My writing group, Under Construction, which meets every Tuesday throughout the school year, has been invaluable to me. Suggesting titles for stories, critiquing content and giving me advice to help me improve my work not only helped, but also made me accountable. So, I need to thank: Lisa Otter Rose, Bridgett Bell Langson, Mary Struble Deery, Lisa Kunkleman, Kim Love Stump, Cheryl Boyer, Jennifer Hurlburt, and Rachelle McClintock. My writing coach and Under Construction instructor, Maureen Ryan Griffin, understands my writing style and has given me the confidence that people will want to read what I write. She is sweetly honest with her advice and patient when I need time to process what she's said. She also edited, designed the layout and helped with original content. Kathy Brown pitched in with editing and was my first reader.

Steve Reisch Photography, located in Asheville, North Carolina, was wonderful in taking me at the last minute for the cover photo and making feel comfortable posing for pictures.

A big thanks to Jack Canfield, who told me that my stories needed to be shared and was willing to give me a testimonial. His vote of confidence was the final push I needed to complete the project. I am now having so much fun, I have started the second book of funny stories. The title is *Fight Naked* and it will be out in 2019.

I also want to thank the many friends and family from Blooming Prairie, Minnesota, who know me and a good many of my stories well. It was a wonderful place to grow up and thrive.

CPSIA information can be obtained
at www.ICGtesting.com
Printed in the USA
BVHW040358201218
536070BV00020B/697/P